# Calls to Mystic Alice

## About the Author

Alice Rose Morgan has been doing psychic readings for more than thirty years. She has read for and helped thousands of people over the years, sometimes several generations of individuals from the same family, and she has hundreds of repeat customers. Her mother was a psychic reader, her husband of fifty-four years assists her with dream interpretations, and all their children and grandchildren have psychic abilities.

# CALLS TO
# MYSTIC ALICE

### A Psychic & Her "Spooks" Explain
### Karma, Reincarnation, and Everything
### Else You Forgot on Your Way to Earth

## ALICE ROSE MORGAN

Llewellyn Publications
Woodbury, Minnesota

First Edition
First Printing, 2006

Book design by Donna Burch
Cover photograph © Philip Harvey / Superstock
Cover design by Gavin Dayton Duffy
Editing by Connie Hill

Llewellyn is a registered trademark of Llewellyn Worldwide, Ltd.

Library of Congress Cataloging-in-Publication Data
Morgan, Alice Rose.
    Calls to mystic Alice : a psychic & her "Spooks" explain karma, reincarnation, and
    everything else you forgot on your way to earth / Alice Rose Morgan. — 1st ed.
       p.   cm.
    ISBN-13: 978-0-7387-0936-9
    ISBN-10: 0-7387-0936-0
    1. Parapsychology.  2. Karma.  3. Reincarnation.  I. Title.

BF1031.M677    2006
133.9'3—dc22                                                          2006045254

Llewellyn Worldwide does not participate in, endorse, or have any authority or responsibility concerning private business transactions between our authors and the public.
    All mail addressed to the author is forwarded but the publisher cannot, unless specifically instructed by the author, give out an address or phone number.
    Any Internet references contained in this work are current at publication time, but the publisher cannot guarantee that a specific location will continue to be maintained. Please refer to the publisher's website for links to authors' websites and other sources.

Llewellyn Publications
A Division of Llewellyn Worldwide, Ltd.
2143 Wooddale Drive, Dept. 0-7387-0936-0
Woodbury, Minnesota 55125-2989, U.S.A.
www.llewellyn.com

Printed in the United States of America

# Contents

**CHAPTER ONE**

## Spooks, Readings, and Reasons ... 1

Who Calls Me   1

"Reading" Defined   3

Accuracy and Privacy in Readings   5

What Readings Reveal   6

Direct Communication   8

A Spook Is ...   10

Why We're Here   12

An Eye for an Eye   14

You're Preparing for the Next Go-Round   16

The Other Psychic in the Family   17

You Are Psychic   19

Why This Book, Now?   19

Psychic Tip: Prove You Are Psychic   20

**CHAPTER TWO**

## Reincarnation and Memories of the Soul ... 21

King Karma   21

Soul Memories: Karmic Echoes of Past Lives   22

Recognize the Purpose of Fears   25

How Our Other Lives Influence Us   28

Children Remember ... for Awhile   31

Childhood "Friends"   35

The Veil of Forgetfulness   37

Psychic Tip: Gather Insights into Karma   38

**CHAPTER THREE**

## The Law of Return, Karma Revisited, and Reflection ... 41

7 x 7 x 7 = Karma   43

Karma Can Be Murky   43

Karma Misunderstood   44

Deception, Dishonesty, and Distrust: Sow It, Reap It   45

Law of Return in Action 46

The Goal: To Understand How Your Actions Affect Others 48

Watch Your Words—and Attitudes 49

Recurring Situations: Karma at Work 52

Reflection: Feedback on Your Efforts 54

Congratulations—You Get to "Wear" the Problem 56

When to Examine Your Behavior 58

Psychic Tip: See the Law of Return in Your Life 58

CHAPTER FOUR

**Death and Dying . . . 61**

Dreams Prepare the Dying 62

My Psychic Roots 65

Dad Communicates from the Other Side 67

Mom's Journey Home 69

Your Loved Ones Are Still Speaking to You 74

Watch for Messages Through Others 75

Watch for Jokes, Too 77

Death Is Really Just the Finish Line 78

Leave a Legacy for the Living 79

Recognize Communication from the Other Side 80

Psychic Tip: Communicate with Loved Ones on the Astral Plane 81

CHAPTER FIVE

**Out-of-Body Experiences and Free Will . . . 83**

The Astral Plane: A Refresher 84

The Astral Plane: Work Zone 84

Plan to Work Out Problems 86

True OBEs 88

You Practice "Dying" Every Night 89

Suicide: Rarely a Good Idea 92

Basic Principle: Free Will 93

Avoid Living Suicide 95

Your Free Will Protects You 96

You Planned Your Life; Keep At It! 97

Psychic Tip: Solve Problems While You Sleep 98

**CHAPTER SIX**

## Attitudes, Affirmations, and a Little Help from Your Friends ... 101

How to Change Your Life  102

Break the Chain of Negative Thought  102

Affirmations in Action  103

Rid Your Life of Butts and Beers  105

The Power of Beliefs  106

You *Can* Teach an Old Dog New Tricks  107

Poor Thinking: Education Comes at a Cost  108

Heed Warnings Well  110

Ask for Help  111

Spooks Do Intervene Upon Occasion  112

Psychic Tip: How to Hear Your Spooks  114

**CHAPTER SEVEN**

## Healing with Color and Alternative Medicine ... 115

Healing Energies  115

Healing Is Self-Healing  116

The Sequence of Colors Matters  117

The Symbolic Side of Injuries or Illness  119

Alternative Healing Methods  120

Alternative Medicine: The Deeper Story  120

Alternative Healing: A Success Story  122

The Right Treatment: Whatever Works for You  122

First: Look for the Cause of the Illness  123

Your Health, Your Choice  127

Healers: Trust Your Skills  129

Quick Remedy: One, Two, Three, Gone  132

Watch Your Language  133

Find the Right Healer  133

Psychic Tip: How to Begin Healing Yourself  134

Psychic Tip: Relate Health to Deeds  134

CHAPTER EIGHT

## Psychic Games, Auras, Energy, and Prayers . . . 137

Play the Marble Game to Find Out Where You're Headed   137

Draw Out Your Character—and Dilemmas   139

Learn to See and Read Auras   140

Energy and Vibrations: A Primer   141

You Pick Up Vibes All the Time   142

Stop the Energy Drain   143

Clean Up Your Aura   145

Cleanse a Room with Salt   146

For Safety's Sake: White Light   146

Employ the Power of Prayer   147

Visualize to Change Your Situation   149

It's Not About the Material World   151

Harness Soul Power   151

Psychic Tip: Teach Yourself to See Auras   152

Psychic Tip: Practice Programming or Praying for Something   153

Psychic Tip: Build Your Psychic Strength by Manipulating Clouds   153

CHAPTER NINE

## Readings and Results . . . 155

The Silver Lining in All Tragedies   155

Looking for Love . . . and Finding It   157

When It's Time to Part, Act   159

Karma Works in Mysterious Ways   161

You Can't Escape Karma   162

Money Sometimes Comes from Unexpected Places   163

In Love, Age Doesn't Matter   164

Leave Another Without Anger   164

Men Are Sensitive Souls   165

Your Gender: Your Choice   168

Watch Your Attitudes   168

Cleaning Up After Charlatans   169

Beware of Roadside Psychics   172

Question Your Own Motives, Too   173

The Best Purpose for a Reading   175

Psychic Tip: Find the Right Psychic   175

**CHAPTER TEN**

# He Loves Me, She Loves Me Not ... 177

Sex ≠ Love   177

Careful Around Those Triggers!   179

Watch the Eyes   180

Eyes Across the Room   181

In Love, Don't Force the Issue   182

Sometimes, Let Her Go   184

Judge Not . . .   184

Maybe You're Not Destined for Love   185

Find Love on the Internet? Fat Chance   186

Fear Will Handcuff You   190

Know When to Fold Your Hand   192

Psychic Tip: How to Find the Love of Your Life   193

**CHAPTER ELEVEN**

# Dreams and What They Mean ... 195

Some Dreams Are Postcards from the Astral Plane   196

Some Dreams Are Precognitive   196

Most Dreams Represent the Working Out of Problems   197

Dreams of Lives Past   198

Dreams Point the Way Toward Spiritual Growth   199

Dreams Recur for a Reason   199

Your Emotions: The Beginning Point of Dream Interpretation   201

The Meaning of Disturbing Dreams   203

Dream Symbols Are Unique   204

Psychic Tip: How to Remember Dreams   210

**CHAPTER TWELVE**

# 9/11, Earthquakes, and Tsunamis ... 213

The Real Tragedy of 9/11   214

There Is No Pain at Death   215

Speak to the Departed 216

The Nature of Natural Disasters 217

Sensing Danger 218

Disasters Pull Us Together 219

The World: Mess or Status Quo? 220

The Coming Cleansing 221

Y2K: Mass Fear 222

To Improve the World: Identify Your Purpose 222

Psychic Tip: Identify Your Purpose in This Go-Round 226

Psychic Tip: Love the Earth 227

# CHAPTER ONE

# Spooks, Readings, and Reasons

Spooks? That is what I call my guides. Others may call them souls, guides, entities, spirits, guardian angels, or channels. I prefer just plain "Spooks," and apparently they don't mind. It's just a friendly, intimate nickname.

I am one of those crazy California psychics, and I have been doing readings in person or by telephone for the past thirty-five years, long before 900 numbers and psychic advertising existed. During this time, I have read for thousands of people from all over this country, including Alaska and Hawaii, and the Bermuda Islands. Many have been clients for years. I have reassured them during the difficult times and shared their pleasure over good fortune or when predicted events came to pass. They know I won't reveal anything we discuss during a reading without their permission. Some have become my friends, others have visited in my home, and a few are now seriously involved in the field of parapsychology. I've even taught some to read cards using the same method I do.

## Who Calls Me

Who is crazy enough to call me? You'd be surprised. I get calls from people in all walks of life, at all levels of education, and in all professions—

possibly even your boss or neighbor. I don't advertise or solicit calls; my name and phone number are passed only by word of mouth. I am constantly surprised by how far and fast that word can spread. All I ask is the person's first name, shuffle my deck of plain old poker cards, and the Spooks do the rest. Yes, I do give the Spooks full credit for the accuracy of the readings. I don't do it; they do. I'm just a grandma, with a favorite hobby of getting muddy in my garden with my grandchildren.

Some of the people I talk to just want to know, "What's going to happen next?" Others want to learn more about karma, the Law of Return, reincarnation, affirmations, and parapsychology in general. (These are just some of the things I'll cover in this book.) Some ask right off the bat, "Are you for real?" My Spooks thereupon give me some bit of information about their personal lives that will help to convince them. One individual I read for was so curious about whether we were for real or not that she drove to California from Minnesota to find out in person. She now works in the field of alternative therapy and is a good friend. Apparently, she decided we were for real!

The most unusual series of calls I ever had the misfortune of receiving were from two personalities in a multiple personality, time-share situation. Both personalities were very strange, intensely disliked each other, and accused each other of spying and meddling. I got hooked on the first phone call, in which the personality rambled on for over two hours. I heard her whole life history. "They" had been after her all of her life. Her story included the love of a mystery man in a "gray flannel suit." It sounded like a bad Grade-B movie, and several times I interrupted to ask if she had written this whole story down—it sounded as if she were reading a script.

This strange call was immediately followed by a call from the other personality inhabiting the body. She wanted an immediate appointment so she could "tell me the real truth about Mary, who is a pathological liar." The second story was just as bizarre as the first! I'm not a psychiatrist, so I tried to convince both personalities to seek professional counseling and the calls stopped after about two weeks.

But that's out of the ordinary. Most callers are normal people with the same concerns you and I have—and the same challenges with work, relationships, and love. Callers relax with me because all I know about them is a first name and the city from which they are calling. I couldn't find them or snitch on them even if I wanted to. It's a pretty safe arrangement for the people calling. By the time they send me a check for the reading with their personal information printed on it, they already know they can trust me.

Some of my clients have been very surprised to find that some of their best friends have been calling me during the same time period, and years may have gone by before one of them admits to the other that he or she has been calling a psychic—me!

Using the telephone for the readings gives anonymity to the caller, but it leaves me wide open to weird phone calls at any time of the day or night. I have been called between two and six A.M. in the morning, usually because people don't remember the time difference in the various zones. Occasionally, I'll get an after-midnight call from some very intoxicated person who just got my name and number from a friend in a bar where they had been happily sharing their grief and problems. I sometimes wonder if my number has been scribbled on some bathroom walls with a "For a good time call . . ." note!

## *"Reading" Defined*

What is a reading and how do I conduct one? Good questions. Let me describe a typical call. Usually, I'll answer the phone and the person will give me his or her first name and the name of the person who referred them to me. We make small talk while I shuffle the cards and spread them out into the reading format I use, typically known as "the wheel." The center card of this wheel usually shows what the individual is "centering" on—what their biggest concern is at that moment. The two lower spokes of the wheel will give me additional or background information, while the other spokes (eight in all) fill in additional information. Say a client asks a specific question, such as, "How is my health?" I locate the eight of spades (the health card) and find which cards touch or are around that card. This usually provides the answer.

In a recent reading, for example, the center card indicated "Divorce, leaving, gone, or over." The lower spokes gave the description of a male with whom she was having problems. I said, "It appears that you are contemplating a divorce or split with a dark-haired man. This is not a sudden decision; it has been going on for some time and you have given it considerable thought." She verified this with an "Oh my God, how did you know?" We then continued with the reading. The various advancing portions of the wheel indicated other things she needed to know that would be happening either to help or hinder her. As with all readings, forewarned is forearmed.

While I get many calls from women regarding the state of their love or marital lives, men form a significant portion of my clientele. One man in particular, whom I've read for a number of years, comes to mind. The first few minutes of the first reading indicated he was contemplating a divorce. His biggest concern by the time he called was that he had just realized his soon-to-be ex-wife was a pathological liar and a chronic gambler. He wanted this validated because he had just found out she also had a new boyfriend. He had bailed her out of a $40,000 gambling debt two years before. Would he be able to get back any of the money that she gambled away? Not likely. Logic and the Spooks said not that money, but they said he would be able to retain and use his future income to his own advantage.

He was very angry, but the Spooks helped him to understand that his ex-wife would owe him in a future life, or that perhaps he owed her this amount from a past incarnation. Only his soul knew which situation really was the basis of the karmic debt. (Don't worry if you don't understand this yet. I'll discuss the nature of such karma and debts in detail in coming chapters.) He needed to let it go, said the Spooks, and get on with this current life without the anger and need for revenge.

He got the divorce and custody of his ten-year-old daughter. He is now buying a new home and will soon be remarried. What's more, he can even be in the same room with the ex-wife now and hold a conversation.

Another man called recently, wanting to schedule another reading. He gave me his name and I immediately remembered that he was a rodeo cowboy who had arthritis in his wrists. I had only read for him once, a year before, and my memory isn't that good, especially when you consider all of the people I talk to and all of the stories I hear. The Spooks helped me remember. (Some individuals comment on my fabulous memory, but I have to give credit to the Spooks. It is not me! When something like this happens, I'm just as surprised as they are.)

The rodeo rider just wanted to thank me and the Spooks for recommending that he try the same alternative medication I use for my arthritis. He had regained the use of his hands and wrists completely, but now wanted to know which direction to take at this moment since several options were open in the rodeo and business world for him. I was able to help him once again.

## *Accuracy and Privacy in Readings*

The accuracy of the readings depends on the individual I am reading for. Usually, the Spooks will offer enough information to convince callers that either I can read their mind or I know someone they know. Neither is true. The thoughts just come into my head. Sometimes I hear a sentence, a phrase, or just a word or two. Occasionally, it is a very vivid impression of the person I am reading for doing something totally out of character as an example of how outrageous their plan is.

A good example just happened. A long-time client was contemplating an audition for an upcoming television show. I had a very clear vision of her wrestling with a large, apelike man for a ticket. This is totally out of character for her; she is a petite, ladylike, talented woman who would never fight in that manner for any material thing in this world. The message: Go to the audition "only if you are willing to fight or get down and get dirty," something she wouldn't do.

I charge $30 for a reading. The amount is the same regardless of the length of time needed to complete the process. Some readings last only thirty minutes, while others continue for several hours. People are on their honor to send me a check after the reading (I don't take credit cards). Nearly all do, since I've only had a few "no pays" in the decades I've been giving readings. If clients ask what I'll do if they don't pay, I say, "If you don't pay your exorcist, you will be repossessed."

If, during the process of the reading, it becomes evident that clients can't afford to pay me, I either tell them they need not pay or can pay me later when their finances improve. The Spooks take care of this too. I have received checks two years after a reading. Some individuals include a tip, if the reading was especially helpful or they feel I could or should have charged more. That is their choice.

What can go wrong? That, too, depends on the client. They have free will and can listen to the advice or not. They can call again or not. I have no way of finding them or telling anyone about them, and wouldn't if I could. The only connection I have with any new client is the person who referred him or her, and I've never asked a referral source about a client. I won't reveal anything that is discussed during a reading with another soul, including with the person who referred the client in the first place.

I maintain confidentiality at all costs for every client. Some have been kind of cute in trying to get information about a friend or relative they referred to me, and the Spooks have helped me to stop the line of questions in a friendly manner. People don't want their personal lives and choices exposed to others, and my Spooks just wouldn't allow it.

## *What Readings Reveal*

I don't understand exactly how the entire reading system works or why a deck of plain old poker cards can help me concentrate or answer specific questions, but they do. Typically, after describing the person and the most serious problem the caller is facing at the present time, my mouth just keeps going until all of their questions are answered—before they even ask them. I tell people in advance to write down their questions before they call so they won't forget some of the important details they want to cover. They are truly surprised when they realize we have covered the entire list, usually in their order of importance.

Often, the purpose of a reading will be to help people get over the rough spots in life until the situation changes and things level out for them, or until the better times the Spooks predict come about. As one of our teachers said, "You get just so many pokes in the nose, and then they give you a box of candy." That's so we'll keep trying and learning. The main thing seems to be that the soul can tolerate anything for a period of time, but we all need to know that there will be a change for the better. That's basically what a reading does. It gives people something to look forward to, offers some suggestions to help change the situation or, if that is not possible, a change in attitude so they can survive and learn.

I often quote the prayer of St. Francis to my callers: "God grant me the serenity to accept the things I cannot change, the courage to change the things I can, and the wisdom to know the difference." It's the "wisdom to know the difference" where we all fall down. I'm sure you remember the times you've jumped in to try to change or prevent an event, which hindsight proved should have been left alone. Being an Aries, I can guarantee I've done it many times.

The Spooks say your soul is learning the most when everything seems hardest, and you are just coasting when life is a breeze. At times, we want to say "Enough already!" But as the Buddha said, "When the student is ready, the teacher is provided." We never know what situation or individual will be our best teacher and our teachers come from some very unexpected sources—such as through me!

Some of my regular callers are other psychics, readers, and astrologers. The Spooks lead them to me when they need clarification on problems in their personal lives or in their readings. Sometimes they just need a little re-direction, verification, and sometimes a good swift mental kick! But then, so do I. It's easy to judge another and forget that person is a beautiful reflection of yourself. Some reflections aren't too nice, and the worse the reflection, the more difficult it is to recognize. We'll go into reflections in another chapter because so much is involved.

It's so easy to let the ego get involved in doing readings, especially when people are telling you how great, accurate, funny, or whatever you are. This seems to be the area all of us who do readings have problems with and this is when a down-to-earth, swift kick seems to be most beneficial. Our Spooks or guides are the ones channeling the information for the individuals who ask for help. We are only transmitters, who through some gift of God are able to receive and forward the help. That is all that we are!

If at any point my ego starts raising its ugly head during a reading, my Spooks can bring me back to reality really fast. The gift just leaves, my mind goes blank, and I'm not sure what my name is, much less the name of the person I am reading for. The Spooks are always right, but sometimes I misinterpret the message or allow my conscious mind to interfere. If I answer with the first thought that comes into my mind, it will be clear. If I have to stop and ponder or try to censor the answer, I've just fouled up!

## Direct Communication

Occasionally, the Spooks use means other than a deck of cards to communicate with me. Sometimes it's through direct mental or verbal communication. When this occurs during a reading it can be a little confusing, because I wonder "Who just said that?" It is even funnier when the client hears it too, and thinks I said something, but it didn't sound like my voice! On one occasion a warning was given to a client in a very definite male voice. My husband Rockie and I both heard it, but it came out of my mouth. It is always a surprise to me and usually is totally unrelated to my conscious thoughts at the time. The communication usually comes as a very strong male voice, just behind my right shoulder, and is so clear I invariably spin around to see "Who said that?"

The first time I heard this type of communication was a little over twenty-nine years ago. My daughter-in-law was pregnant with my oldest grandson, and we were standing in her bathroom talking while I did my hair. She turned to a side profile in the mirror, viewing her belly at its full eighth-month size, and said, "Isn't that gross? Isn't that obscene?"

After she left the room, I wrestled with my hair while thinking about her poor baby's reaction to that statement. I was already very much involved in parapsychology, and I knew the soul would already be connected to the unborn child and would be aware of what was said or done in its presence. Being a typical grandmother, I was hoping the soul understood that nothing personal was intended by the remark when, over my right shoulder, a clearly masculine voice said, "Well, frankly, I think it's a little obscene too, but it's the only way to get here." Startled, I looked up in the mirror and spun around, fully expecting to find my son or husband standing behind me. No one was there, and I realized my future grandson had just talked to me. I started laughing, thinking how completely opposite this communication had been from the path my conscious mind was taking at that moment. I immediately went into the other room and informed my son and daughter-in-law that they were definitely having a boy and told them what had just happened. (The boy who spoke to me in utero, by the way, received his doctorate in Planetary Geology from Brown University in April 2005. He is very intelligent, reserved, and serious, and he's just as clever and witty today as he was the day I first heard him speak.)

When this type of message comes to me, it may be related to my conscious thought, but it always throws me an unexpected twist and can't be ignored. Other times I will just hear one sentence with no connection to current activity or ideas. The message in the sentence will nearly always be revealed during the next few hours and will prove to be precognition or a message to teach me.

Once, while driving to work, for example, I'd been struggling with trying to decide if I should just throw in the sponge and give up on a particular job and make a change. While my mind ran around in circles with all the pros and cons, my Spooks suddenly said, very clearly, "Do you want to exchange three months for three years?" Three months later, the problem resolved itself. If I had forced the issue at that moment it may have been another three years, but who knows?

Before you decide this book is dedicated to the "Wonderfulness of Myself," let me assure you, it's not. No matter how much we learn or how much good we can do, it is still a learning process until the day we die and even beyond. Just about the time I think I have some problem all figured out, under control, and "I'll never do that again," the Spooks give me a test that I have proven I can flunk just as fast as the next person. It's usually so obvious I can't miss it.

One good example was the battle I had with cancer on my back. I jokingly asked the doctor if I could just keep my melanoma for a couple of more weeks until it was more convenient to have it removed. He said "If it is a melanoma, you might just as well keep it for good. It won't matter anyway." He was suggesting a funeral might be in order.

Well, it was a melanoma and that was twelve years ago. Guess what? I'm still here.

Why cancer at that point in my life? I had been teaching others that cancer is often caused by internalized anger and frustration; and a problem with the back often indicates that you're carrying a burden. Both of these things were true for me at that time, but it never occurred to me that I could cause or allow cancer to happen to myself. I don't think I would have chosen cancer to play games with since most of my family dies from cancer or complications. The Spooks certainly got my attention. I'm sure you have discovered in your daily lives that some of the wisest souls can do some pretty dumb things.

## *A Spook Is . . .*

A Spook is a soul just like us, who is not currently incarnated or inhabiting a physical body. The Spooks I refer to throughout this book are my guides, guardians, angels, or some of the master teachers from my own soul group who choose to offer their help on the earth plane at this time. A Spook can be a soul with the same level of understanding as you—although with the broader perspective and wisdom that comes with full-time residence on the astral plane—or it can be a higher self, a wiser, more knowledgeable you, with all of your memories intact.

Sometimes a soul or a Spook with specific knowledge is allowed to give me information or speak through me to advise in a special situation.

I mentioned "soul group" just above. This is an important concept to understand, because it explains so much. Not just reincarnation, but . . . God.

Try to visualize a beautiful, swirling mass of sparkling colors in a huge, clear, distant galaxy that you can see into. That is God, or our energy source, whatever you choose to call it. From that beautiful swirling energy comes a great fiber optic tree trunk rising up and out into branches, twigs, and leaves. We are the leaves, our soul group is the twig. Our goal is to return as one to the beginning swirling mass of God.

We increase the strength and perfection of the source with the knowledge we gain through our experiences. It is an old saying that, "There is nothing new under the sun." Perhaps not, but we can improve the beauty and power of our own particular galaxy, which is why we keep trying.

Our individual souls began existence and chose to work together with others at the same time, very long ago by earth time. (The Spooks say time on the astral plane is very different than earth. Approximately twenty-four hours on the astral plane is equivalent to one thousand years on earth. This is one of the reasons it is so difficult to give exact time to clients when they insist on it.)

Why groups of souls? Much more can be accomplished by the strength and energy of a group working toward the same goal than can be accomplished by individuals working separately. As time progressed, some in your group of individual souls learned the lessons early and well. They became master teachers to help others progress faster—just as we have professors and specialists here on earth. They are the senior members of our group, but still part of our group. They cannot and do not force us to return to earth, but can help us decide in what direction our souls need to go to complete our cycle and improve the entire group.

If we choose not to incarnate on earth, we don't have to. But we are shown the options and choices. Our teachers and guides help us make the decision, but the final choice is still ours. It just takes a lot longer for us to complete the learning process if we stay only on the astral plane, and most of us are impatient creatures. We want to return to God or the Universal Consciousness, or whatever you choose to call the source from which we emanate, and we want to return as a group.

We have probably all come along as Spooks for others in our soul groups—we tend to travel together—as they've incarnated in the world. Or we will in the future. You want to work with your own group whenever possible for the good and advancement of the entire group. According to the Spooks, we each progress at our own pace but really want to stay together whenever possible. It's like having your family, soul mates, or best friends with you all of the time—and we all know that sometimes they can be very trying. That's how we learn! When

I tell my Spooks "I'm trying," the response is usually "You certainly are!"

## *Why We're Here*

We're on this planet to learn. Our souls chose to incarnate into various physical bodies during various times to learn certain things. (Yes, you have lived before, perhaps many times. More on this in succeeding chapters.) The earth is a beautiful planet and the human body has evolved to be uniquely suited to the psychic body or soul. We are able to realign quite easily to life here; it's something we do every morning after our nightly trip "home."

Your soul knows what you have come to work on. And much of what you experience has been planned before you were even born, so there really are no surprises. The only surprise is your reaction to the situation when you are confronted with all of the emotion involved in learning.

Our souls also chose to incarnate into other dimensions and areas of the universe to gain specific knowledge. I am not really able to understand these different planes or bodies yet. Maybe I will be given more information before I leave this life, if it is something I need to know.

Learning is a really interesting process. We usually choose to learn the hard way, and we learn best from our own mistakes. If we choose to learn from observation or accept the knowledge given us by older and wiser souls, life could be much easier. The fact is that most of us choose the School of Hard Knocks.

For instance, assume you are a new young soul, just dying to get down to that wonderful asylum called earth to learn all about life. God grants your wish, brings you to earth, and says, "You will be here for eighty years. I want you to observe all that is happening and at the end of that time I'll be back to get you."

At the end of the eighty years, God returns and asks what you have learned. You are bubbling over with excitement, "Well, I saw this happening, so I did that. Then someone else was doing this and it was new to me so I tried it too and . . ." You rattle on and on.

God just stands there, shaking his head, and finally says, "I told you to observe, not to do. Had you only watched you would have learned and been free of this experience. Now you will have to go back and undo all of the things you have done." So we return, again and again, until we learn.

Once we commit to a lifetime of action rather than observation, we need and choose to learn by physically experiencing all phases of the particular problem. A good example would be sex. How many souls can really learn by just watching? Only the wisest souls are able to choose the easier road and learn just by observing, but they have already moved up and away from the earthly plane and no longer need to reincarnate here. Most of us chose the action because we sincerely believed we would have been wiser than the souls who just observe. Remember that ugly little ego? That probably has more to do with our choices than anything.

We can learn by observation, but because free will is involved, we chose the harder path. On our first incarnation on earth, we chose to live by experience and now must complete the cycle until we finish with the earth experience.

Imagine your soul starting out as a sparkling clean drinking glass. On the first trip we add a little gray gunk, the next incarnation we get rid of part of that mess, but we add more of another type until we end up with a heaving mass, overflowing the glass. As we slowly learn, we gradually remove more dirt until at last the glass is clean and we don't need to return to the earth again. By that time, the soul is much older, wiser, and would like nothing better than to graduate to the next plane or learning center.

## *An Eye for an Eye*

There's another reason we must come back to earth again and again. Every emotion and problem we cause another soul to endure, we then must experience. As the Bible states, "An eye for an eye, and a tooth for a tooth." You need to repay not only the individual soul that you harmed, but understand and experience the pain others who loved or cared for that soul went through because of your actions. This is so we learn completely and will never be responsible for causing the same hurt or turmoil again.

For example, in the process of overcoming our emotions of anger, hate, and fear, we may have murdered another soul and cut short his or her opportunity to learn. We then must come back and be killed, losing lifetime opportunities of our own. In another lifetime, we may have to experience the anguish felt by people who lost a loved one through the senseless act of murder, and in perhaps another, feel the guilt and remorse left with friends and relatives who felt they could have prevented you from committing the first murder. To understand completely what our original act sets in motion, the hurt and pain involved, we have to experience every phase of it—even to the point of being put into a position of wanting to kill again, but stopping yourself, thereby stopping the wheel that would continue turning until your soul learns.

This may sound like a far-out hypothesis to you, but when you look at world history, all of us must have been capable of murder at some point in our soul's past. Thank God, most of us have evolved past that stage to the point where it is the exception, rather than the rule.

This doesn't mean that you will have exactly the same experience, but it will cause the same emotional reaction in you that you caused another to endure. Since we are all individuals and walking our own paths, our reactions to a situation are different. What might really upset another person, you might take in stride, and wonder why others can't handle the problem as easily. That's why I love the old Indian saying "Don't judge another man until you walk a mile in his moccasins." The Bible also states, "Judge not, lest you be judged"—same message. We are each learning what our own soul needs, in our own way. We really have no way of knowing exactly where another soul stands on their road at that moment. Others have lived in situations totally foreign to you and have different strengths and weaknesses.

An example of my own problem in judging others is a situation that came up during a reading not long ago. I had just finished a reading for a woman who was having a great deal of worry and stress due to her son having lost his foot in an automobile accident. We discussed the whole problem and she realized she was reacting with more concern than her seven-year-old son—who was busy proving the loss of one foot wouldn't stop him. The Spooks also wanted her to know that her son would be chosen in a special experimental program for people with artificial limbs and he would help himself and many others as a result.

The very next phone call was from a woman whose main concern was when she would be able to find a compatible bridge partner! My immediate reaction was, "What? You've got to be kidding!" then I promptly heard my Spooks reminding me not to judge. The problem was as real to her as it was unreal to me, and I worked to keep my conscious mind from distorting the information the Spooks had for her. Oddly enough, that question was just a nervous starting point for a soul whom I was happy to know and help for years. She did many good, kind, and charitable things, helping many people in many ways. The bridge club really didn't matter that much to her, either. It was just a form of relaxation in an otherwise very busy, productive life.

Keeping the conscious mind from censoring material has been one of the hardest things to learn in using my psychic ability. If I stop to think about the information the Spooks are channeling or start thinking "That's not logical," I can totally misdirect the channel. I've found my "reading self" being very understanding, helpful, and sympathetic in some situations when my "normal self" would like to give the person a good, swift kick. Not that the Spooks don't forward some pretty tough advice at times. They do.

## You're Preparing for the Next Go-Round

The Spooks tell me the earth is the hardest learning center in the Universe, sort of the "Insane Asylum of the Universe," according to one very wise man. One step above earth, the physical plane, is the astral plane. This is the heaven of Christian beliefs. The astral plane is where our souls rest between incarnations, where we review our failures and triumphs in our most recent and previous sojourns to earth, and decide in what areas we need further education. The Spooks say there are many more planes and dimensions beyond the astral plane, some we can't comprehend from where we are right now.

Not that the time in the astral is spent lying around thinking of the error of our ways or patting ourselves on the back. The Spooks teach that life on the astral plane is much like life on earth, but without the pain and suffering. The desire for knowledge and the more positive emotions remain with us, the memory of all past life experiences is very clear and we don't go around asking, as we do on earth, "Why am I here?" We know why.

On the astral plane, you remember all of your past lives, successes, failures, or experiences that helped you to become who you are now. On the earth plane, however, the "veil of forgetfulness" is drawn, usually by the time you are six, because it would be too difficult to live this life with the total soul memories of everyone you had loved and lost in prior lifetimes. It would be overwhelming for any individual to have all of these memories and still be able to function during a current lifetime.

What if you remembered the one you loved most bleeding to death in your arms? What if you had been involved in the Holocaust with all of the horrors and could remember all the pain and losses? Doing past life regressions is extremely traumatic and can be very stressful to your current body. Soul memories should only be researched with great care.

As mentioned, we have souls with whom we are very close, and not in relationships such as we have on earth but much more intense. We actually reincarnate with a group of souls and choose to remain together as long as possible. (Your soul mates are thus all around you right now!)

On the astral plane, we work, learn, and counsel other souls who are coming and going, and start in motion our plans for our next earth education experience. That's right, we set our own stage, arrange the sets and the other actors, and then wait for the right set of circumstances so that we can all be born in the right sequence to work on our problems. So the next time someone says, "I didn't ask to be born!" the response is, "Yes, you did. You arranged the whole scene."

You also plan when you'll die, but that becomes part of the planning you forget when you incarnate on the earth plane. What if you knew how long you would live, even to the exact hour and day because you planned it? Typically, if we know the outcome, we will try to get by with as little effort as possible until the last minute, or try to find a way to get out of the commitment. One lady I read for called two weeks after the reading, very upset because I had told her that her husband would die in two months or two years. I wasn't sure, but it was definitely two. She was very angry when he died in two weeks. When I asked her what the difference would have been, she replied rather sheepishly, "Well, if I had known it would only be two weeks, I would have treated him nicer." I rest my case!

All this may not be concepts you would like to accept, because it means you have to assume full responsibility for your actions. There is no one else to blame. This rather blows holes in the "Poor Me" routines some people make part of their lives or the "Why did God (or the Devil) do this to poor, sweet, innocent little me?" Every time I catch myself thinking "Why me, God?" the Spooks immediately answer "Why not? You asked for it!" Even if you honestly feel you have done nothing in this lifetime to deserve what you are experiencing, it may very well be a lesson you need to learn as a result of behavior in a previous life.

## The Other Psychic in the Family

The Spooks aren't the only help I have in this life. I have the great fortune to be married to one of the most truly wise and patient souls alive today. Rockie and I have been married for fifty-four years. He is just as involved in the psychic field as I am, but in a different area. He does hypnotherapy and past life regressions for people and has a real gift for dream interpretations. He often joins me in a reading to help interpret a dream that is particularly puzzling for an individual, and he often helps me understand my own dreams. Being psychic for others doesn't necessarily mean you can be psychic for yourself or for your own family, and Rockie often helps me accept this. At times, just the emotion of caring too much prevents me from receiving the information the Spooks are sending, especially if I really don't want to hear any bad news. Being a Libra, Rockie has always been my balance wheel and has kept my Aries self from going off on a wild goose chase more than once.

One whole chapter in this book will be devoted to examples of Rockie interpreting dreams for people with particular problems. The dream knowledge comes from inside himself and has not been aided in any way by various books on dream interpretations available on the market today.

Rockie is my partner in many other ways. He quite often schedules my telephone readings. That's a blessing—it helps him understand what is being accomplished and thus tolerate a wife who sits with one ear attached to the phone, dealing cards every night! We also work together on radio talk shows, teaching individuals and small groups and once taught a class in parapsychology at a high school.

That proved to be a memorable experience. At the end of the lecture, during the question-and-answer session, we found ourselves reading palms for over sixty students. The funny part was that we had agreed to read palms, thinking we would split the class and it wouldn't take too long. Some two hours later we still had students waiting in line. We then discovered that the little characters were checking up on our accuracy by having both of us read for them separately and then comparing the results! They were also bringing friends in out of the corridors to have readings on their lunch hours. I realized what was happening when some of the students started saying, "Gee, that's what Rockie just said." We were being conned, but we were also being accurate.

Rockie and I also discovered that we had to be extremely careful in accepting invitations to parties. Some people invited us as the evening's entertainment. Doing readings is fun, but can be very tiring, especially when you are doing them one after the other for large numbers of people for hours.

When I say "we" or "us" in this book, I mean Rockie and I.

## *You Are Psychic*

We all have the gift or ability to read. It's just a matter of allowing it to develop and trusting it. I've been able to prove this to some of my clients during their readings by asking them specific questions regarding my appearance, number of children, or other information. Usually I tell them not to think, or try to use any logical deductions. Just answer with the first thing that comes to mind. They have really been amazed at what their own minds are capable of.

One of my regular clients was discussing her recently deceased grandmother with me, not being sure if she was really receiving communication from the other side. Just for fun we did a test during which I asked her to describe my mother, who was also on the other side. This time, I was the one really surprised. She described my mother perfectly, then said, "Oh yes, something about rose or rose colored. I don't quite understand." My maiden name had been Rose, and everyone had called my mother "Grandma Roses." I was not using my maiden name at that point, and there was no way she could have known this without help from some type of extra sensory perception. She realized she had much more psychic talent than she thought.

You're psychic, too. To prove it to yourself, see the tip at the end of this chapter.

## *Why This Book, Now?*

Why am I writing this book? I realized long ago that much of the advice that helps those I read for would be helpful to others. Because I can't read for everyone, my Spooks insisted that I write this book. It has been fun to share some of my personal experiences in learning about the paranormal, the results of predictions I make during readings, answers to the "Big" questions of life, and how we all can bounce back from setbacks, overcome challenges, and take advantage of opportunities. Often, I am truly amazed at the accuracy of the information given through me. At other times my conscious mind is just as amazed at what my mouth is saying.

But you be the judge of that. Let's begin.

**PSYCHIC TIP: PROVE YOU ARE PSYCHIC**

Find a friend, and just let your minds relax. Then take turns asking surprise questions that the other person couldn't possibly know about someone you know who is no longer on earth. Answer whatever thought comes into your head. You'll both be surprised by some of the answers.

Throughout this book, I'll have little exercises like this one for you to do. Keep an open mind, and you'll begin to awaken your own psychic abilities.

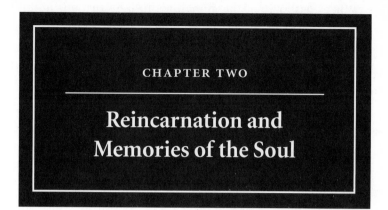

# CHAPTER TWO

# Reincarnation and Memories of the Soul

According to the Spooks, a soul never has to come to earth if it chooses not to, but since the learning opportunities are so great here, and since we can progress so much faster, most of us choose this experience. Again and again.

Fortunately, we have a lot of help learning. The people you meet in life, especially the people you are close to, are usually souls you chose to come into this life with. It also may include people you think of as enemies—and these are people you can learn from as well. We are all related; some through positive experiences, and others through negative experiences. Put another way, we interact with our soul mates and others with whom we have positive and negative karma.

## *King Karma*

Karma plays a big part in your life. Anything you love, hate, fear, or desire too much is often a reflection of your karma. Karma can be a debt or it can be a credit, either a minus or a plus carried over from past lives. You may "owe" somebody for having done that person many wrongs, or that person may owe you for ill treatment or for the good deeds you did in another life. Fears are often karmic, as you'll see, because they are connected to deaths, bodily harm, illnesses, and other karmic events.

People often ask me in readings, "What's my karma?" Only you can answer that question by being honest about the situations in this life that bother or delight you the most. Some of our experiences in past lives leave such strong impressions that we are born with fragments of memory or fears we can't explain, and abilities and knowledge beyond what we have learned in the current lifetime.

Many individuals don't want to admit to anyone what these specific feelings and memories mean for them. Some may involve incidents that happened during this life, such as molestation, that they aren't sure happened or would rather not get involved in, so they choose to forget. If people actually do remember, they might choose not to tell anyone. This is their choice. As you'll see, "As you sow, so shall you reap." Who wants to admit they really started the problem?

Karma isn't all negative. It can be reflected in positive things—wealth or talent or lovers or helpmeets who chose to find each other and continue a life on the earth together, perhaps to provide a special home for some of their soul group.

Rockie and I, for example, believe creating a "special home" was our choice for people from our soul group: our children and grandchildren. Each person in our lives has their own special mission or plan, but each needed the positive reinforcement this lifestyle provided. Many of our children's friends commented on what unusual parents we were and how lucky the children were. (I'm not sure they agreed, and certainly not all the time!)

In the next chapter, we'll put a sharper point on karma and what it means for you.

## Soul Memories: Karmic Echoes of Past Lives

Inexplicable things happening in our children's lives pushed Rockie and me into learning about parapsychology in the late 1960s. Unexplainable events and abilities related to children are among the clearest hints we have that reincarnation, karma, and psychic ability are real and affect our lives. When our oldest son, Rockie Jr., was in high school, for example, he was able to tell us who would be calling and what the message would be before the phone would ring. We really thought this was a gimmick cooked up by Rockie Jr. and his friends until Rockie Sr. got a call from the California Air National Guard where he was employed full time to notify him that the unit was about to be activated due to a national emergency. They couldn't have set that one up! Rockie Jr. just got pale and said "Dad, it's for you, an emergency." Our younger son Mark was a natural pilot and able to locate any object that was missing, just by concentrating. Our daughter Debbi was a natural healer and could write what resembled psalms from the Old Testament with her eyes closed, the pencil moving at an unbelievable speed, with words we had to look up to understand. At first we thought it was all a hoax to drive the old folks nuts, but we met other parents who were experiencing similar situations in their lives. It could make you extremely nervous, especially when so many teenagers were on drugs at that time. This wasn't drugs; it was real—and unexplained by conventional knowledge.

The abilities and fears of our children were not just fascinating, but ultimately revealing. From birth, Debbi was deathly afraid of worms, to the point of becoming totally irrational if someone threw a worm at her, if one was found in an ear of corn we were cleaning, or if she dug one up by accident. No amount of logic or reasoning could convince her that worms couldn't and wouldn't harm her. (Of course, I could see how unreasonable she was because her fear wasn't like my fear of frogs. Worms don't jump in erratic directions, don't have large mouths, and are much smaller. Now, I ask you, how rational is this? You can see I was a great help as a mother!)

Her fear continued on through junior high school, when her teacher threatened to fail her in biology if she did not dissect a worm. He had no idea how deeply seated this fear was or that her reaction would be so traumatic the day she walked into the class and found the worms waiting. She was sent to the nurse's office, and I was called to take her home. The teacher apologized repeatedly; he said he had assumed it was just one of those teenage "girl things."

When Debbi was a young woman, she decided to clear this fear so she wouldn't become a hysterical mess when her children discovered nice little earthworms and brought her their treasure. She also wanted to clear the problem due to a childhood memory of her own that involved a hysterical mother who came totally unglued when she and her younger brother had brought a beautiful, big, fat bullfrog into the kitchen to share with me. They had no idea I was afraid of frogs and were unprepared for my reaction, which was to climb the wall backwards screaming like a fishwife to "get that monster out of here." I can still see the shocked look on their faces.

Being an older, wiser soul than I, she went to a hypnotherapist who did past life regressions to help her deal with this fear. During the regression, Debbi found herself in a past life as a small boy, quite ill. People around her were dead or dying, and black, slimy worms were stuck on her body. Through asking her questions and moving back and forth in that time period, and with a lot of calming reassurance, the therapist was able to discern that she was apparently in England during the black plague. Many people died, and physicians decided that using leeches might in some way help plague victims. Debbi was treated with leeches and survived the experience, but she was left with the abnormal fear of leeches and worms of all kinds, which she connected with suffering and sickness in this life.

Knowing the source of the fear helped—she doesn't become irrational at the mention of worms any longer—but she still hasn't been able to deliberately touch one.

Debbi is now a nurse practitioner with a master's degree in nursing, just at a time when science has decided there may be a medical use for leeches after all and they are starting to be used again. I have to wonder if our Spooks have a twisted sense of humor. Makes you wonder!

My frogs? Well, I still haven't willingly touched one yet, but my Spooks have arranged a few cute little surprises for me. Like stepping on one with bare feet out in the garden, leaping ten feet straight up in the air, and flying to the porch. (That was how the neighbors described my reaction.) I know intellectually that frogs can't hurt me, but the emotional and physical reaction is still the same. Every hair on my body stands on end, a rush of adrenaline speeds through me along with an overwhelming fear, and I don't think. I just react.

I'm not over this fear yet, but I'm getting better. Where the fear comes from is not connected to anything in this life. It is completely irrational, and I have never investigated the source. I'm sure it is deeply rooted in some past life experience.

## *Recognize the Purpose of Fears*

My Spooks tell me the source of the fear is immaterial. The importance is to recognize that many people have similar fears, just as irrational, but every bit as real. Some of their fears can really be disabling and these are the fears people need help with. Apparently, my stubborn soul wouldn't really understand without experiencing a form of the fear, so I have to live with this irrational and silly phobia in order to help others.

Remembering and understanding—that's why there is a need for fear. Fear starts a physical reaction in your body and activates the flight-or-fight syndrome that was needed to survive on this planet in the past. Some of our fears come from serious and dangerous situations we encountered in a past life. Some of our fears, particularly the irrational fears, are just memories your soul has retained from some experience during a previous life, usually something very traumatic but not necessarily life-threatening.

I don't think my frogs were traumatic, but who knows? Maybe I drowned in a flood and the last physical thing I remember was a frog. The frog was not responsible in anyway, but just stuck in my memory as an omen of something very frightening or life threatening, just like Debbi's worms.

The irrational fear doesn't really do you any good now, but is just a strange reminder of a previous existence. The point is, fears in this life often have their roots in past experiences. When you can recognize that the fear is from a past lifetime, you can understand it and gradually let it go. The fear itself can't harm us, but it certainly makes us behave in strange ways.

Not all vivid soul memories reflect karmic events. One way to know the difference: karma usually requires an action on your part in response. Also, karma keeps being repeated in various ways until you learn the lesson and will give the correct response every time, not just when you think of it. A soul memory won't necessarily require a response, other than, "What was that all about?"

Fearsome past life experiences that cause physical problems in the present are quite common. Not long ago, for instance, I read for a young woman who was extremely allergic to cats. During a regression to a past life she saw herself as a three-year-old girl on a farm in the Western United States. She had been told not to leave the house or go into the barn, because it was extremely dangerous for some reason. Of course, being a child and a curious little soul, she immediately went out to the barn, where she discovered a box of baby kittens. She was delighted with the kittens, petting and loving them. In the process, however, all of the kittens spilled out of the box and one accidentally scratched her. She started crying and running to the house with all of the kittens playfully following her. In her mind, they became the danger she had been warned of and they were chasing her to cause further harm. By the time her imagination finished embroidering the episode, she was firmly convinced the kittens were a pack of fierce lions intent on having her for their next meal. She was punished for her disobedience, which helped to enforce the hurt and fear. She then completely blocked the entire experience from her conscious mind and hated cats from that point on, not knowing why.

After finding where the reaction to cats came from, she was able to laugh at the fears of a tiny three-year-old from a previous life and cleared the allergy in this lifetime.

Psychologists are now beginning to use hypnosis and past-life regression techniques in working with patients to find the basis for many individual problems. They find, as I do, that some of our fears are based on childhood memories, others in past life experiences or, in some cases, a combination of both. Some are more intense than others, but we all have them and they are very real to us, even though some may be just as irrational as my frogs.

As my cat-fearing client proved, however, an attempt to understand the cause of an illness or phobia can clear up the problem—sometimes overnight.

My youngest son has a very strong soul memory of burning to death, while his wife has an abnormal fear of earthquakes from a past life. When you put this combination together you can get some pretty bizarre situations. When they were first married, my son had a very vivid dream in which he was on fire and was flapping his arms in an attempt to put out the flames. He was not only dreaming, but was apparently also walking and yelling in his sleep. He woke to find his new bride running around the apartment yelling, "Earthquake! Earthquake!" In his half-awake state he asked her why she was yelling earthquake when he was on fire? He had jumped out of bed, shouting and throwing himself about the room in his sleep, which had awakened her. He was yelling "Fire," but she heard "Earthquake," and each was responding to their biggest fear. I can only imagine what the neighbors in the apartment house thought since this happened at about two o'clock in the morning.

My daughter-in-law went to the same hypnotherapist as my daughter Debbi for a regression to help her understand her fear of earthquakes, or at least overcome part of her fear, since they were living in the Bay Area in California. She also felt uncomfortable in large crowds and was fearful that people would start screaming and running after her.

During the session, everything became very clear. She was a child, standing next to a very large building when an earthquake occurred. A huge crowd was running wildly in terror toward her, trying to escape the destruction, with church bells ringing as a result of the quake. The building she was standing near for protection collapsed and she was crushed in the rubble.

This left her with her combined fears of earthquakes and crowds—and even bells. Any sudden ringing noise, like a bell or phone, had always startled her and she had avoided being near any exceptionally large man-made structure, such as the hangar at Moffett Field, where her husband was stationed at the time. She had gone out of her way to avoid large buildings and crowds all of her life, without knowing why.

It had never even occurred to me that bells, anchored in church bell towers, would undoubtedly ring during an earthquake, at least until the tower fell. Soul memories come up with strange, and strangely logical, information.

## *How Our Other Lives Influence Us*

My youngest son is a natural pilot and knew how to fly before he even climbed into a cockpit. Once, he went on a field trip to a nearby Air Force Base with a group of Boy Scouts when he was about fourteen years old. During the visit, each boy was allowed a turn in the flight simulator. When Mark's turn came, he knew what all of the controls were, took off, flew the simulator, and made a perfect landing, much to the surprise of the airmen operating the equipment. Not too long after that, he started taking flying lessons with a local flying school. The same story—he was a natural.

About this time he told us about a dream, or some kind of memory, in which he was a pilot during World War II. He said he was a pilot for the RAF in England. He felt he was not English, but came from Norway or one of the Scandinavian countries. He insisted that he knew what New York looked like from the air back then, and that he came over with a group of other pilots to fly some American planes back to England. He later became a test pilot for the RAF and died in flames while testing a plane. My response at the time was "Just a bad dream. You won't crash and burn, so forget it."

You can imagine my reaction when I read the whole story he was relating in Herman Wouk's *Winds of War* twenty years later. In it, he describes the "Lend-Lease" program before the U.S. entered the war. Yep—fliers would come over here, get planes, and fly them back to England.

When our oldest son was five, he came down with rheumatic fever. During one of the attacks he was out of his head with a very high fever. He was talking in a strange adult voice and kept saying, "I don't like this earth. I'm going to leave this earth!" He repeated this over and over with a great deal of anger and forcefulness. Needless to say, we were scared out of our wits, particularly when he didn't appear to recognize us and his eyes were wild and angry. All the while we were driving the thirty miles to the nearest town to get medical help for him,

I held him in my arms, trying to calm and comfort him. Periodically, he would raise himself up and look at one of us very intently, shudder, shake his head, and lie down again. Whatever he was seeing in us was very unpleasant to him and he wouldn't answer when we tried to talk to him. Of course our imaginations didn't help the situation, especially as he stared at the moon intently the rest of the time. By the time we got to the doctor, we weren't sure if we had a little "Martian" on our hands or what.

This was fifty-two years ago, and Rockie Jr. did not attend school yet. We did not have television and the children had few playmates or outside contacts. How could a five-year-old refer to this planet as Earth? He may have known the word "world," but not "earth." After that he became very interested in science and space. It was an experience we never forgot and he didn't remember at all. Apparently his soul really did not like to return to this earth at that time. Perhaps his master teachers and others in the soul group encouraged him to at least try to complete the necessary lifetime to learn the lessons our souls needed.

Remember: A lifetime on earth allows us to learn so much and is really a very short time on the astral plane. From the astral plane, we can see all of the possibilities. That usually helps us make the right choice for our soul's advancement. It's like watching a movie running into the future giving the variables based on the choices you make. When you know your soul is in control and has the power, your fear of advancing is reduced. The Spooks say it really is just a matter of "choices," your choices.

But back to Rockie Jr. When he was a senior in high school, he decided he really wanted to learn to play the piano. We thought he was a little old to start, but agreed we would buy an old upright if he could find an inexpensive one. Since we thought this was just a passing fancy, we didn't want to make any long-term, large investment. His prior experience had been twelve organ lessons when he was fourteen, at which time the kids decided to trade the organ for a pool table.

He started teaching himself, and within six months was playing Beethoven's "Moonlight Sonata" and several other classical works perfectly. He was particularly fond of Beethoven's music and his self-taught ability was astounding. When he decided he wanted to take music lessons, we agreed. He went to a local music teacher who said she wasn't able to teach him any more than he already knew and referred him to a concert pianist. When he played for the concert pianist, she wanted to know where he had learned his "phrasing." He didn't even know what that term meant. She then told Rockie he played the music the way Beethoven had written it to be played, that she had never heard quite that interpretation, and that she could have him on the concert stage in two years if he wanted that career. She also warned him that it was a very lonely life and took a great deal of dedication, but he did have the skill. This is when we bought him the conservatory grand piano, which he still owns and plays even though he decided against a musical career.

Rockie's older children both play classical piano and violin but learned over a number of years, taking lessons as people normally do. They did not have instant ability. His two younger sons are both taking lessons now and are very good. Some of the greatest musicians in history seemed to know music almost from birth and were playing before they were five years old. The Spooks say it is a memory from a past lifetime. The only thing holding back the ability of such geniuses is the willingness to practice with the hands and physical body that the soul is currently inhabiting until you have the necessary manual dexterity required to play.

Rockie Jr. has also always had an interest in Germany, both the language and the people. He was fluent in German by the time he started college. An exchange student from Germany was in one of his classes and was firmly convinced Rockie Jr. had been raised in Germany, since he spoke the language with an accent common to a particular area. You guessed it—it was the area that Beethoven was from. I asked a friend of mine who does past life readings to see if it was possible my son was Beethoven reincarnated. Now, I think people who are determined to believe they or a child was someone of great historical significance in a previous life are amusing. It is what you learn and the good you do during a lifetime that is important, not who you were. Still, I had to wonder.

It seems Rockie was not the great composer but, as the psychic put it, one of Beethoven's peers who had lived during the same time frame in the same area, knew Beethoven, played and loved the music, and studied under him. Rockie's abilities and knowledge helped to convince us in our belief in reincarnation, and the soul's ability to retain skills and memories from past life experience.

## *Children Remember . . . for Awhile*

Our daughter, Debbi, has been able to do automatic writing since she was about twenty years old. She has communicated with her children while pregnant with them and found the information obtained is very accurate. Watching her write is absolutely fascinating. The pen moves so fast it seems impossible that any human being could write at that speed.

Debbi used this means to pick the very unusual first name given to her oldest son, Jebediah, then chose her father's middle name, Jay, to be the baby's middle name.

Also, from communications prior to birth, Debbi knew Jeb would be a boy, what he would look like, and his choice for his name. He even gave her the spelling, since it is a very unusual name. The soul who was to be her son also stated that his soul name was "Morgan," and that he liked the name. She asked through automatic writing if the baby wanted his name to be "Morgan," to which he responded that he thought "Morgan Morgan" would be a little redundant.

When he was less than two years, he legally changed that middle name in the process of being adopted by my daughter's husband. He was almost two, but had been walking at seven months and was able to hold a full conversation at one year. He was very precocious.

During the proceedings, the judge asked if Jeb understood what adoption was and if he was in agreement. When the judge was satisfied with the response, he announced that Jeb's legal name would be Jebediah Jay Hall from that time forward. At this point, this tiny twenty-two-month-old baby interrupted with, "No, Judge, that's not right!" Startled at being corrected by a two-year-old, the judge asked what was wrong. Jeb then told the judge that "Morgan" would be his middle name. The judge chuckled and said, "So be it! Your name will be Jebediah Morgan Hall." It wouldn't have mattered to an average two-year-old, but the name did matter to the soul who had returned in that body. For his own reasons, he kept a name that was important to him.

Another unusual situation concerning children was our family's experience with a darling three-year-old girl named Lacy, for whom we babysat on different occasions. I worked with Lacy's mother, and she had told me of Lacy's bad dreams. Several times the child had awoken during the night upset. Her mother asked, "Lacy, what's wrong?" She replied, "I am not Lacy." When questioned further about her identity, she would say, "I won't tell you who I am. You don't need to know."

According to her mother, Lacy's voice, expressions, and general be-havior was very similar to our son's at five when he told us he "didn't like this earth." It was frightening. Neither of us could figure out the meaning and managed to thoroughly confuse and scare ourselves, es-pecially since *The Exorcist* was a hit movie at the time.

One evening when Lacy was leaving our home, she was in her mother's arms at the door when our oldest son started down the stairs and muttered something to her in German, a language he was quite fluent in by then. Lacy immediately twisted around in her mother's arms, glared at Rockie Jr., and said, "I am not a bad girl." At this point, my son practically fell down the remaining stairs, looking stunned. I asked him what had happened. With a very bewildered look on his face he told us he had just said, "Don't go out the door, bad girl," to her in German, and she had responded correctly in English!

Our younger son was babysitting one evening and called us for help. He was a little nervous about Lacy's behavior; she would cor-rect his errors in German grammar, giggle, and run down the hall. She not only understood German, but she was able to speak the language as well. All of these instances were completely spontaneous on Lacy's part and we were not able to question her about any portion of it. If we tried, she appeared not to know what we were talking about and denied any knowledge of what that "funny talking" meant.

One of the biggest clues we got into Lacy's past life memory came when our daughter and her boyfriend were driving across town with Lacy in the car. Several blocks ahead of them, a police car had pulled someone over to the curb with the lights flashing and the siren just running down. Lacy suddenly became very frightened, started crying, screaming something, and trying to get out of the car. They stopped to calm her down. She was screaming hysterically that the police would burn her, and that they had burned her babies! Nothing would ease her mind, so they made a U-turn and took a different route home. They were all very upset by the whole affair. Lacy, with dried tears on her cheeks, didn't seem to know why she had been crying, but could remember that she didn't like police; they were "bad."

On another occasion she was watching television with her mother, some child's Western with Indians and other children—nothing particularly frightening—when she started crying. When her mother asked her what was wrong, she said, "They burned my babies. The police threw them on the fire." There were no police in the movie they were watching and no one was in danger of being burned to death!

It would seem from all the soul memories Lacy was having that she was very likely remembering some portion of what is now called the Holocaust. She was undoubtedly in a German camp for the Jews, lost her children, her family and her own life. Why the strong, frightening memories at the age of three? I don't know, but the Spooks say she came back to the physical plane too quickly. She didn't take time to recover and understand on the astral plane.

Perhaps some memory this bad can only be worked out on the physical plane. So much has been revealed about that era in the past twenty years that perhaps the healing can occur on the earth plane with the others who were involved. Lacy is about forty years old now, and I've lost contact with her family, but I wouldn't want to discuss it with her. She was about twelve when I last talked to her, had no conscious memory of what she was able to recall from a past life at so young an age, and I wouldn't want to try to remind her or regress her into that past life. The memories would be too painful.

I have heard of other young people with strong memories, bad dreams, or some knowledge of the World War II era above and beyond what they may have learned from the news media. My son's memory of being a pilot in the RAF and another young man who is firmly convinced he was a Kamikaze pilot in the Japanese air force are but two examples. Emotions attached to the story and the feelings connected to that bit of history seem to be the outstanding difference between imagination and memory. The Spooks say, "Your imagination isn't that good!" We human beings have very active imaginations, but we usually are able to control how far we will let our responses go. Imagination rarely carries strong emotion and physical responses such as sweating, shaking, crying, or irrational fear.

It helps to understand that any particular life was just one of many. Some may come with extraordinary memories and "baggage," but it is still just one of hundreds. That should help put such memories into perspective.

Many children between the ages of three and six can often recall incidents from other lives. At those ages, children can communicate well enough to tell us of the memories, but are not yet old enough to have the "veil of forgetfulness" completely drawn. I've discussed and explained many of these situations with parents or grandparents in readings.

One of our grandsons sat in the back seat of the car and told his parents all about living a lifetime in the desert. He was only four years old and probably wasn't consciously aware of where or what a desert was; they lived near the ocean in Alameda at the time. Yet, his facts were unbelievably accurate. Another of our grandsons sat at the dinner table calmly eating his dinner and telling us, in a very matter-of-fact voice, about his grandchildren. When I tried to get him to continue, he looked up at me, his eyes went blank and he had no idea what I was talking about! The memory left just as quickly as if someone had turned out a light.

The next time one of your children or grandchildren starts telling some "story," listen. You may be very surprised at what you learn. We have found these tales have some very accurate facts that a child of that age couldn't know and are always spontaneous on the part of the child.

In other words, you can't con or force information about soul memories out of a child. If you try, they just forget.

## *Childhood "Friends"*

One other interesting situation with children and the psychic realm is their ability to see things we can't see. Everyone has heard of children who have imaginary playmates. Adults get all upset and make appointments with psychiatrists or child psychologists to stop this embarrassing nonsense. Usually the children outgrow the need for the spiritual playmate and no longer see them, but sometimes the ghost friend is still there when they grow up, as one of their guides or Spooks. The children who do continue to see a friend just learn not to talk about it and gradually lose the ability to see into the other side, or astral plane. Attitudes and what we have been forced to learn and accept destroy the natural psychic ability that every soul is born with.

Our oldest grandchildren had two "friends" when they were under four years old. The one with them most was apparently a little soul similar to Casper, "the Friendly Ghost." They called him "Georgie Ghost" and he was very real to them. We had to move over to make room for him in the car, be careful not to sit on him or knock him down, and in general treat that bit of empty space as it if was being occupied by another human being. Their other friend was "Big Georgie." They were a little afraid of him, but also knew he would protect them and Little Georgie. I have no idea what this was all about or why, and concern for Georgie gradually disappeared after they were four. They both became perfectly normal teenagers (if there is such a thing) and were both in graduate school obtaining their doctorates, one in chemistry and the other in planetary geology. (They can't be too mentally impaired!)

They don't even remember Georgie except for what we have told them. They were only fourteen months apart and weren't lonely or neglected in any way. They just had some extra friends. We just acted like Georgie was acceptable and as real to us as he was to them, and no one was ever concerned.

Children also seem to be able to see a future event that we may not want to see. My nephew and his children were visiting us one afternoon when we lived with my mother and we suddenly decided to go to the cemetery where my father is buried. Everyone was standing by the graveside, basically just visiting and reminiscing, when my nephew's four-year-old looked up at my mother and said, "You're next, Gramma." His father reprimanded him for saying such a terrible thing, but he was right. Mom died about six months later. We all heard what he said, but Mom interpreted it differently and said, "That's right. My place is right here next to Grandpa." Small children know these things with no conscious thought of upsetting anyone. He had no idea what he had said or what it meant.

My granddaughter was "busy helping me" load the dishwasher when she was about two, when she stopped, looked at me very seriously and said, "Grandma, you are going to die." My thought was, "Is it soon? She is too young to even think of death. Why did she say that?" Then she giggled and said, "But it's OK because you get to come back and be a cute little tiny baby again." This was said in a squeaky little tiny voice that rose at the end of the sentence. She was very happy for me. Here, I was hoping I'd never have to come back to this earth again! Oh well, maybe later I'll want to. She has no memory of any part of this exchange.

When our daughter was living in her husband's family home in Alameda, she also became aware of her two-year-old son's ability to see souls from the other side. She had been aware of another presence in the home at times, but thought she was the only one seeing and feeling something. One day, her son asked her about the "dark-haired lady" he had seen in the upstairs hallway on different occasions. He then proceeded to describe his other grandmother, who had lived and died in that house from cancer years before he was born. He was even able to pick her out of a picture of a group of people.

I have been doing readings for a friend, Kelly, for a number of years, and she has shared experiences she has had with her sister, who has Down's syndrome. Her sister is in her late twenties, is becoming more independent as time goes by, and is doing very well. She is a very loving and trusting soul who can be surprisingly wise and intuitive at times. Her sister tells Kelly about talking to and seeing their grandmother and uncles who have been dead for quite a while. Apparently her sister has tried to discuss this ability with other members of the family, but has learned they think this is very odd and they make her feel uncomfortable about it, so she only talks to Kelly about it now. I have told Kelly to listen to her sister because it is very probable that she is still able to reach souls on the other side, just as small children seem to be able to do. It seems to be related to childlike faith and trust, which most of us have lost long ago.

## *The Veil of Forgetfulness*

The Spooks say that a soul has to have the veil of forgetfulness drawn so that we may really grow and learn from our current experience on earth. Some are born with no obvious soul memories, others seem to gradually lose the memory between the age of three and six years. Some of us regain the ability to remember portions of past lives if the knowledge could be beneficial, or we can recall and use a skill developed in a prior life. My Spooks say I have been a psychic reader and teacher in many past lives and that I must continue.

My daughter says that when she was little, she always felt disoriented and confused when she first woke up. She felt that she had just left what was real and this world was the dream. I know she was always difficult to awaken and was a grump for the first hour. Now we know why—she didn't want to come back here. Two of her sons have felt the same sensation, especially when they were younger.

If we were able to remember all past lives, loves, deaths, and problems, we would not be able to survive; the daily stress of living here is more than enough to cope with. Remembering all our past loves and losses would be too much. Our life on earth would also seem less real and we would not learn from enduring the emotions we came to experience.

Our existence during a lifetime on earth seems the most important thing in the universe while we are alive. We will do whatever is necessary to preserve and prolong this life. We are supposed to feel this way in order to be willing to stay our full, allotted time and learn the most from the experience. When we die and return to the astral plane, our whole physical life seems to have been very short and is more like a strange, but very educational dream. The negative emotions we were learning from on earth are gone and only love remains. We return to the astral plane to resume our soul's quest for knowledge and to re-unite with those who have gone before, and who gather as a reception committee at our death. I know who many of the members of my own committee will be right now and I'll be delighted to see them again.

Try to keep in mind that your entire life is an education that you have personally chosen to fill in the missing pieces of emotion and un-derstanding your soul needs. No other soul is involved in these choices; only you.

---

### PSYCHIC TIP: GATHER INSIGHTS INTO KARMA

You can understand much about your other lives and the lessons you're here to work on, but you have to be completely honest with yourself. To begin, write down the things you love, hate, fear, or desire the most.

How do you feel when confronted with one of these situations? Can you face it down or does it make you want to run? Once you know what you are working on, it becomes much easier to recognize the karmic tests when they are presented and to give the proper response.

Another way to investigate your karmic ties to other lives is to recall particular memories or recurring dreams from your childhood. Write down as much detail as you can and try to figure out what it means. If you're quiet enough, your own Spooks will add some insight. Some memories are very obvious, others more obscure. What emotion does talking about it evoke? How does it make you feel?

Finally, listen to small children when they appear to be telling a tall tale or just a story not related to their present life. Write it down. They may tell you more at another time. Do not punish or correct a child's statement during one of these episodes. You may not know what you are talking about, and they do!

# CHAPTER THREE

# The Law of Return, Karma Revisited, and Reflection

For every action, there is a reaction. It's one of the laws of physics and definitely one of the most important laws of the universe. This is the basis of what the Spooks call the Law of Return. Whatever you put out comes back to you, positive or negative. The Bible puts it this way: "As you sow, so shall you reap."

Each time we do something negative, the action will return to us, usually within a short period of time. The purpose of this is to give us the opportunity to see the fruits of our mistakes. The problem is, we're stubborn. We try very hard to ignore the consequences of our behavior. We think maybe just this one time we can get away with it, but the Law of Return never lets you get away with anything until it becomes karmic. And when a problem becomes karmic, you get to wear it for as many lifetimes as necessary to learn.

A good example of this would be stealing or taking something from another soul or group. The first time you steal, you get away with it from all outside appearances. But then something is taken from you, either through theft, loss, or destruction. It may even be the item you stole in the first place. You don't see any relationship, so you steal again, then lose again. Each time you take something, you feel less conscious fear and become more bold, taking and losing more each time until you finally make the connection. You steal a car, your car is stolen. You steal a car and sell it, your car is totaled in an accident and the insurance just ran out. Your Spooks, a group that includes your higher self—the real you—can be very creative and can get really rough trying to teach you.

You can watch the Law of Return in action and see the effect immediately with small children. Often one child will hit another, turn to run away from retaliation or punishment, only to trip, fall, and be hurt worse. The Law of Return thus starts when you are a very small child, continues throughout all of our lives, and is one of the ways the universe has of educating us. Return can come through inanimate objects, animals, or from other souls, but it is always there.

The Law of Return and karma have a very positive side also, which quite often we see and don't recognize. A good example: the hardworking, deserving person who wins the lottery after buying only one ticket, while the rest of us spend money every week, just sure our number will come up. Some people, by the way, call me wanting to know what numbers to pick, what game to play in Reno and will they win? I have to laugh because the Spooks won't let me do that. I can't even pick numbers for myself or my family.

Sometimes the Law of Return is so exact, it is unbelievable. Approximately fifteen years ago, Rockie and I gave $500 to someone who was really desperate. We knew he would never be able repay it, so we just made it a gift, no strings attached. At that time we could afford it, but we didn't make a habit of giving money away. About ten years later, we received a check for exactly $500 from a totally unexpected source—and at a time when we desperately needed the money. We hadn't asked for it or tried to borrow money, and no one associated with the giver had any idea we were short of funds at that time. I called to thank the people, told them the story of the exact amount returned from a totally different source, and told them the same thing would happen to them in the future. They said it gave them goose bumps!

## 7 x 7 x 7 = Karma

The Spooks say we are allowed to make the same mistake seven times seven times seven, or 343 times in a lifetime, before it becomes karmic. (Not including things like murder, which is of a different order. According to the Spooks, murder is a disastrous mistake, because you affect so many lives.) We are given plenty of opportunity to see the error of our ways. Once we have passed that point, we have built a karmic debt that we will have to carry for as many lives as necessary to clear it.

By the way, none of us is an innocent bystander when karma or the Law of Return are involved. If something is stolen from you, you can bet either one is involved, or it's time for an important lesson.

One lady I read for called from the parking lot of a shopping center in tears. Her car had just been stolen. I laughed and told her she needed a new car and didn't want to buy one, so her Spooks took care of it for her. After a short conversation we determined that her car was nine years old, had started requiring very expensive repairs, and she was trying to be thrifty. She had enough in her savings account to buy many new cars and her car was insured; she just didn't want to spend the money. She ended up laughing and said I always made her look at things from a different point of view.

She loves her new car and the one that was stolen never turned up. The Spooks say it was taken by a ring of car thieves and went across the border into Mexico within hours of the theft. It just added another layer to the huge karmic debt that ring is creating. I know that my client never stole an automobile in this lifetime or a previous lifetime, but I know she got a lesson in the value of material things and when to let it go.

## Karma Can Be Murky

Karma sometimes appears inexplicable. We have all met the wonderful guy next door who is honest as the day is long, but he gets robbed every time he turns around. No one else on the block loses a thing, but he gets hit over and over. It just doesn't seem fair and is totally illogical. If you put karma into the picture and consider the fact that he may be repaying a karmic debt and learning in the process, then it starts to make a little more sense.

After a lifetime of losing everything you try to accumulate through criminal means, your soul is given the opportunity to steal again in its next life. If you have learned the lesson, you won't touch a thing that is not yours. If you haven't learned, you start the wheel in motion all over again.

I once read for a man who found a wallet on the sidewalk with almost $1,000 in cash inside. No one was near at the time, and he could have just pocketed the money and thrown the wallet away, but he just couldn't do that. As far as he was concerned, this would still be stealing because it didn't belong to him. He debated turning the wallet in, but decided he would try to contact the owner of the wallet personally. He thought he might be able to get it to the owner faster, since it might otherwise be tied up for weeks in the legal system. When he did, he discovered the money was all the man's savings, which he had just withdrawn to pay his wife's hospital bill. The owner of the wallet had been frantic and so appreciative he wanted to give my client a reward. My client refused the reward but felt really good about his honesty in returning the money.

He didn't have to return it. He could have gotten away with it on the physical plane. But he knew that sooner or later he would have to pay it back. He believes in the Law of Return and karma, and says, "I know if I ever lose my wallet, someone will return it!"

Without a doubt, he had apparently been on the theft-and-loss roller coaster long enough and had learned the lesson thoroughly. I told him he could be very proud of himself. He had just completed a very important lesson.

## *Karma Misunderstood*

Some very unusual attitudes exist in the way some Eastern Religions view karma and reincarnation. The Spooks say the original teachings of the great masters have been changed.

The Spooks say that a human soul always returns as a human and never is incarnated as an animal or inanimate object. That belief would involve transmigration of souls and could only happen under very unusual circumstances involving a great deal of very difficult karma. In other words you can't be a tree, a cow, or any other object or animal.

I do remember reading a real cute story years ago about a man who hated and mistreated dogs, only to find himself in a dog's body. He learned to be an extremely good dog, his only fault being that he hated all mail carriers. As the dog lay dying, after doing a heroic act, his only thought was that he would probably have to come back as a postman.

The other difference between what the Spooks say and some other beliefs is the fatalistic attitude about karma that some cultures express. In India for instance, some people will see a person drowning and think, "Oh well, that must be his karma," and ignore the situation. What if it was your karma to walk by at that moment, be in a position to help the drowning person, and you chose to ignore the entire situation? You have to ask yourself, when is it your responsibility to respond and help, and when should you only observe? I think the time to just observe passed for each of us long ago. The answer lies in the Golden Rule, but we all have to make that decision for ourselves.

## *Deception, Dishonesty, and Distrust: Sow It, Reap It*

The same laws apply to emotions and feelings. If you hurt another person in some love relationship, such as pretending to love, then dropping the pretense as soon as a better situation comes along, the same thing will happen to you. Some of the people I've read for can't understand why they can't find someone who truly loves them, when a little honest introspection shows they have been very thoughtless of other people's feelings in past relationships. Sometimes just a "remember how it felt" is all that is needed to remind them. Sometimes the threat or promise from our Spooks of having to do it all over again is enough to make a thoughtless soul think twice.

When we are young and just starting to learn about love and sex, we are self-centered and thoughtless. We have all fallen in and out of love, but we don't understand how much it can hurt until something—like getting jilted unexpectedly—happens to us personally. Most people gradually learn from their own mistakes and become more emotionally mature, less self-centered, and more concerned for the other person's happiness. However, it seems that some individuals take forever to learn. But learn we must, even if it does takes forever!

Love is the strongest emotion in the world and in the astral plane. It is the basis of all of the great religions existing on earth today. If we could just live by the Golden Rule, "Do unto others as you would have them do unto you," we wouldn't face any of the problems the world faces today. Now it seems most people live by, "Do others before they do you." Worse, many aren't even aware that that is their attitude.

## *Law of Return in Action*

One man I know has been very busy with the Law of Return over the past few years, and I am hoping he will see that the cause of his problems lies in his own actions. I can't point it out to him, unless he were to ask, which is very unlikely. He is too busy feeling sorry for himself.

Larry started out in the business world after returning from the service a little mad at everyone. He gradually worked his way up the corporate ladder to a management position. He hired and fired at will, giving little thought to the burdens and problems he was causing for others. He activated the Law of Return, and he himself was fired. Still roaming around with a chip on his shoulder, he had a great deal of trouble getting another job and ended up going into business for himself.

Once again he was in trouble because, as a business owner, he could hire and fire, and treat the employees as badly as they would accept before quitting. Soon his business was in big financial trouble. He lost it and went to work for another corporation, starting at the bottom. Being a very diligent employee, he once again climbed up the ladder of success and into the management area. But since he had not learned from his previous experiences with power, he again hired and fired at will, at times firing people for very unfair reasons and with absolutely no consideration for the emotional and financial harm he was doing to the employees or their families.

In the process, he made a large group of serious enemies, some of whom would love to see him dead, and some who would like to help arrange it!

After about two years in the management position, he was finally fired unfairly, or at least for all the wrong reasons. This time he spent over six months looking for work before he was able to find a job, putting a great deal of emotional and financial strain on his family. This was, of course, the same burden he had put on the various employees' families in the past. The Law of Return involved the family members to try to help him understand the impact his actions had on others. If he couldn't see the impact on himself, at least he would see it on his loved ones.

I'm sure that with his intelligence and abilities, Larry will ultimately end up in management again. I hope he has learned to treat employees with more consideration and respect, and doesn't let his cold handling of power take over again. If he has not learned from his own past experiences, the wheel will continue throughout this lifetime until it becomes karmic in his next. His actions have already caused so much unhappiness, and each reaction to him is worse than the previous one.

At some time in the future, perhaps something will finally get through to Larry, but probably not until it happens to his own son or daughter. Often we can't see the pain we are causing others until it comes home to roost and injures someone we love. Otherwise, we are stubborn enough to continue the same behavior right through all of the tests presented by the Law of Return and create the karma. We are able to find so many excuses for our behavior. Power and the need to control others is one of the things we all have to work on, and most of us need to get "beat over the head" again and again before we learn. This is why so many individuals are still on such a power trip in the world today.

## The Goal: To Understand How Your Actions Affect Others

Several of the women I read for have similar problems with karma and/or the Law of Return. They were adopted as tiny babies, grew to be young women who in turn had daughters out of wedlock and were forced to give them up for adoption. They know how it feels to be an adopted child with all of the unanswered questions. They also know how it feels to be the mother who suffered the loss of having to give a baby away.

One case in particular, which I have been following for some time, is a lady I'll call Gayle. When Gayle first called me, one of her biggest concerns was if and when she would ever find her real mother. She had been adopted as an infant by a couple who had six sons and had wanted a daughter all of their lives. Gayle loved this family, but she wanted to know who she really was and why she'd been given up for adoption.

We talked about it for a while, until the Spooks offered her this message: "Open both doors." It didn't make sense to me until she finally admitted that she gave birth to a daughter prior to her marriage and put the baby up for adoption. She didn't intend to tell me even though my Spooks had picked up the existence of four children, while she insisted she only had three.

Apparently, she had never told her husband about the affair and adopted baby, and she didn't want to ever let him know, even though they were now in the process of getting a divorce. She feared he would use it against her to take full custody of their children.

The Spooks reassured her that it wasn't important to tell him, now or ever, since he wasn't the adopted child's father, but that she must open both doors. When she did, she would find her mother within six months.

She went through the divorce, finally registered her name with a service that allows adopted children access to information if they want to find a parent. She opened that door. She then obtained the information about her mother from another source within six months, just as predicted. The Spooks had warned her not to be disappointed when she met her other family, since only some of her questions would be answered.

Gayle arranged to meet her birth mother. When she did, she understood the Spooks' warning. She really didn't like the woman who had given birth to her and concluded quickly that she was a pathological liar. Every story she told Gayle contradicted a previous one. Of her newfound brothers and sisters, only one loves her, and she maintains contact with him. The rest of her birth family were and remain strangers.

Gayle is still not able to find out why she was put up for adoption, while the parents kept the others. She heard too many conflicting stories by various members of the family. At this point, she is just grateful she was put up for adoption and raised in the loving situation her adoptive family gave her. The one thing Gayle knows is that when her daughter decides to find her, she will tell her the truth, love her, and hope that she will understand.

The situation Gayle found is not typical. Most of the women I talk to really want to find their children. They want to come to know them, remember their birthdays, worry about their welfare. Attitudes toward unwed mothers even twenty years ago were pretty bad. The option of keeping a baby when you were a young teenage girl didn't exist. It still isn't easy, but now it can be done, even though a lot of pressure is put on the individual to allow an adoption.

## Watch Your Words—and Attitudes

This brings me to my own little Law of Return/karma mess, for which I have no one to blame but myself.

I can remember saying, as a very small child, "Next time I'm going to be a boy!" I've always felt I got cheated by being born a female, and I was firmly convinced somebody got mixed up and just gave me the wrong plumbing. Boys had all the fun, got away with everything, were paid more, had neater toys, etc. My parents were so old-fashioned that they believed a girl shouldn't ride a bicycle, didn't want me to learn, and refused to buy me one, even though all of my brothers had them. It just wasn't ladylike. (Who ever said I was a lady?)

I really wasn't happy with the prospect of marriage and didn't want anything to do with childbirth—mine or that of anyone else. Even at seventeen, I stood at my sister's bedroom door, telling her the morning sickness was all in her head and when I got pregnant I just simply wasn't going to have it! One year later I was married, pregnant, and guess who had morning sickness? That's right—morning, noon, and night for five months! Followed by back pains, muscle cramps in the legs, and one month of glorious false labor for every one of my three pregnancies. The Law of Return was in full force. Everything I thought or said about another pregnant woman I got back in spades. Now I began to have some inkling as to why I didn't want to be a female.

Along with the fun of having babies came another little present that came with the territory of being female in my family: congenital, hormonal migraine headaches. Horrible headaches that last two to four days each and came twice a month as our hormone balance changed in our bodies. I had the first one at twenty and they continued each month until I was fifty.

When I got involved in parapsychology, I decided to find out about the source of this problem and went to see a hypnotherapist. The therapist told me there was no such thing as a migraine headache with a karmic origin, and mine was due to current attitudes. (Well, I've been known to have an attitude.)

During the session, I wasn't really sure I was actually under hypnosis until my mouth started saying things I couldn't control. The story that evolved, partially under hypnosis, and the remainder in automatic writing from the therapist's Spooks, is one I'm not proud of. But it's one I have to work on.

It seems my soul usually prefers to be a male when incarnated in the flesh, to the point that I had to be strongly encouraged to accept a female role by wiser souls from the other side. It seems sooner or later a soul needs to learn the role of both sexes and I had procrastinated long enough. It was time and I reluctantly agreed. During one of my past lifetimes, I was a man and also a doctor, which explains why I knew anatomy before I even took the class and why I've always been interested in medicine.

As a doctor in that life, I had no understanding of women's female problems, and I thought childbirth was simple and women were just big babies when they experienced any pain and discomfort. I apparently had no understanding, and no sympathy or compassion, in treating female patients. I was thoughtless, cold, and cruel. To ensure that I would never forget, the Spooks not only made me be a female, playing a typical women's role, but also helped me figure out a means of being reminded every month with a migraine. Then I also got to watch my daughter start having them at nine years of age. I had already seen both my sister and my mother suffer from these disabling headaches, and later several of my nieces. It is a very strong congenital trait, but then we are also all very strong, determined women with an apparent karmic tie.

When I came out of the hypnosis, I could vividly remember some of the things I had said and the attitudes I had carried when younger. Since that time, I have actively tried to change my thoughts as well as my actions. Some women are fortunate in feeling well during a pregnancy, looking pretty, and having babies in a reasonable period of time. My daughter and I had miserable pregnancies, complications, and we looked like hell and felt worse. It is bad enough to go through your own problems, but it hurts just as much to see a daughter suffer. I know this is also her own karmic problem, not just mine, but it doesn't make it any easier.

The hypnotherapist was really surprised, since this was truly a karmic migraine. Even though I knew the source, I was unable to do anything about it until I reached menopause. Believe me, I tried, but I usually managed to make things worse.

Another interesting fact came out of that session: I was not only a doctor in that life, but an alcoholic one at that! Nice guy, right? I have hardly been able to drink an alcoholic beverage in this life. I allow myself one glass, but if I take a second, I immediately get a pounding migraine and become sick to my stomach. I've only been intoxicated once, and that was when I was in my late twenties. We had been to a family housewarming party, and when I did not get sick on the second drink, I decided to push my luck with a third. The next morning, I awoke so sick I thought I would die—and I wanted to. It was Cub Scout Sunday and, being a den mother with fourteen Cub Scouts, I had to pull myself together and take them to church. I know we were only in the church for one hour and I spent half of that time in the lady's room, but it seemed like several lifetimes. I ended up in the hospital for five days, drinking milk and taking medications to deal with the ruptured blood vessels in my stomach.

I must be an extremely stupid, stubborn soul, because my Spooks arrange things that are hard to forget. Needless to say, I'm totally cured of drinking in this life.

Another aspct of alcoholiism is the effect on the family of the alcoholic. They endure the worry, pain, and guilt, not sure how to handle the alcoholic. We have a tendency toward alcoholism on both sides of our family. In that way, I've also been exposed to watching people I really care for going through the hell of an alcoholic's experience. I know it is an illness and a chemical imbalance that makes some individuals more susceptible than others, but karma is usually involved also. I just pray that I've learned all of the sides of this problem and won't choose to get back on that merry-go-round in my next lifetime.

## *Recurring Situations: Karma at Work*

You know you're dealing with karma and/or the Law of Return when situations continue to show up in your life. For example, my older brother has a phobia about the noise made by motorcycles, particularly young people racing around with dirt bikes, totally oblivious to the rest of the world. He has already moved three times, because he always ends up in an area where the noise level drives him to distraction. The funny thing is that no matter how carefully he picks the new home location or how thoroughly he checks out the neighborhood, the noisy machines follow him. It is very frustrating to him and the rest of us can't help but wonder what his karmic thing is with these aggravating noise levels. He will hear motorcycles when others don't even notice. Who knows? Maybe he helped to invent the gasoline engine or the motorcycle in another lifetime and had no consideration for the complaints of others.

My husband had a similar noise disturbance problem for years. He couldn't stand children crying, fussing, or fighting at the dinner table, something all children do from time to time. The funny thing is, we couldn't even go to the nicest, most expensive and adult restaurant in town without having someone come in with a baby or small child, sit at the next table, and start the karmic disturbance. It even happened in Hawaiian nightclubs where no one would expect to find children. Once he looked at the problem from the standpoint of karma, and started laughing about it while he picked which group of screaming children would probably be put at the table next to us, the problem stopped.

When it's no longer a problem and you are able to see it more clearly and laugh about it, you don't have to work on it anymore.

So how did this disruptive-child thing ever get started for Rockie? The Spooks say that it started in his life as a Mormon with twelve wives and all of the assorted children from those relationships. (This gives me a migraine just thinking of it.) That number of children behaving like saints would still seem disruptive! It would certainly try the patience and Rockie has those soul memories. He is very good with children, but can also be pretty impatient with cranky, fussing children, as we all are.

He says—to add insult to injury—he was also a teacher in that life and had children other than his own to teach.

When we first started to notice the uproar in restaurants it was upsetting until we realized it was happening too often to be just a coincidence, and started trying to understand what and why. During a hypnosis session, Rockie discovered the karmic details, and we were able to understand and laugh about it when it occurred later. It may also explain why we seemed to have so many single women who had lost their husbands come into our life needing help and friendship. Maybe some were his wives from that life.

## Reflection: Feedback on Your Efforts

Rockie and I feel that it is important to give whatever we are able and sometimes a little more. We find that if you are loving, kind, and giving, you are surrounded by people of the same nature. If you are a user and a taker, on the other hand, you will be used and what you want most will be taken from you.

Sometimes, no matter how hard you try, the positive side just doesn't seem to be coming back. Don't give up. You may still be repaying debts from a previous life. You will catch up. It is the Law of Return and reflections around us that give us the opportunity to see our mistakes and correct them before they become a lifetime of karmic misery.

One lady I have read for is really a good person who goes out of her way to help others all of the time. She takes cooked meals to sick friends, gives rides to others even if it means going a long distance out of her way, and never accepts payment or gas money. She just feels this is how friends should behave.

Several times she has called almost in tears because the circumstances had been reversed and she needed help, but no one offered it. She honestly believes in the Law of Return, but can't understand why she is always expected to give. She was so upset by the greedy, thoughtless people around her that she had just about decided to quit being Mrs. Nice Guy. It just didn't pay.

When questioned, she admitted that the friends always thanked her and acted like they appreciated her help, but never offered to reciprocate. She also admitted that she never asked anyone for help or let them know she needed it. She thought they should be able to figure it out for themselves!

The Spooks reminded her that she was still building up a large stockpile of positive returns that would come back to her at some time in the future. She admitted she really couldn't quit helping her friends and neighbors—she just wished they didn't always expect her to jump in and take over. But she was so good at it!

We also discussed the possibility that she owed them from a past lifetime and it was time to return favors done for her before.

Shortly after this conversation, she needed minor surgery. She was totally overwhelmed by the way all of these people rallied around and helped with everything from cooking and housekeeping to childcare and transportation. They were pleased and happy to help her when she obviously needed help and was not in a position to argue. Most of them weren't being greedy or selfish. They just thought she was so perfect and efficient she didn't need anyone. Remember—she never let people know she needed them, too, so she didn't give them the opportunity to return the favor. When she really needed them, they came through. What you sow, you reap! She got a bumper crop and quit keeping score. Sometimes, just keeping track of "who owes what" causes a problem, so drop the score card. Give, and let your Spooks take care of the return.

But for most people, if you look, you will see your behavior reflected in the behavior of others around you. Quite often it's someone that you just can't stand to be around, but if you look honestly and closely, you'll see yourself doing and saying the same things. When the same personality type keeps popping up in your life, look closely. Maybe your behavior isn't quite as inappropriate, but perhaps it is a very large reflection of something you need to work on. The Spooks often exaggerate a problem so we will be forced to acknowledge it.

One reflection that most people miss are the politicians that we elect to office, our representatives. The word "representatives" tells it all. We elect those individuals who best represent the biggest majority of the people in our country. So if we have elected officials who are dishonest, greedy, power hungry, and lazy—look around you. How many people in your area behave just like their representatives? The opposite would also be true, but how often do we hear people complaining because politicians are too honest, modest, or considerate? Those who represent us are our greatest reflection.

Two of my grandsons are Aries, like me. One of them has a birthday only two days from mine. Talk about a reflection! I can see myself as a child doing and saying the same "Me first!" things he does. When another grandson was born an Aries, I realized I apparently needed more reflections in seeing myself as a selfish, ego-oriented child. People born under the sign of Aries have some very good aspects, but the large piece of ego is a negative trait that needs to be worked on and put into proper perspective.

Two of our other grandchildren are Libras, like Rockie, so there apparently is a need for him to see the reflection of himself in them. This works both ways and a positive reflection of what you can become is often helpful. How often have you gotten two of your friends or acquaintances together, thinking they will get along great since they are so much alike, only to find they instantly hate each other? You can see the similarities in behavior and attitudes so clearly, yet they are insulted because you would even suggest such a thing. They are not ready to recognize the reflection and won't even admit the possibility.

You can also see this in families where adult children will carry the same attitudes and behavior of a parent they have never gotten along with. They will often even look alike but really resent anyone mentioning the resemblance. One young man I know looks, sounds, and acts just like the father he hates and can't understand.

## Congratulations—You Get to "Wear" the Problem

One of the areas where we are all aware of attitude problems is in driving. Many news articles have been written about how the perfectly peaceful, kind person becomes a raving homicidal maniac when put behind the wheel of a car. The next time you start getting really upset in traffic, think. That "damn fool" in front of you may be a beautiful reflection of your past or present behavior. A little courtesy, friendliness, and a large change in attitude could contribute a great deal to safety on the highways. You don't have to be responsible for teaching every crazy driver a personal lesson by retaliating, getting revenge, and "showing them how it feels." Try the other approach: Let someone cut in the line of traffic or have the parking place. Wave a hand instead of just one finger and you'll see the same response coming to you. Again, the Golden Rule.

I've never been in a hurry in a grocery checkout line that someone hasn't offered to let me go ahead, but then I always let others go first when they are obviously in a hurry or only have a few items. Courtesy and friendliness pays off every day, but when I've been thoughtless or inconsiderate I've also had that immediate return. Sometimes I've become so involved with and pleased with watching a Law of Return in action that my attitude gets twisted and then the Spooks let me wear a little of the problem so I won't enjoy it so much.

Some years ago I was working with a young man who was the company superintendent and could be very hard on the people working under him. He was seldom sick and really couldn't understand why people thought they had to take time off when they were ill. One afternoon, I sat at my desk watching and listening as he ranted and raved to the other supervisor and one of the owners about those "sickly weaklings" staying home from work, causing him so many management problems.

It was winter and a particularly difficult virus was working its way through the company. I couldn't believe what I was hearing, particularly when Don had apparently forgotten that the two people he was blowing off steam to were both just recovering from the same flu. One had been off work for a week when his flu had turned into pneumonia and the other had missed several days at the peak of his illness. Both had returned to work before they were really physically able and as a result were trying to work and recuperate at the same time. I saw them exchange looks several times while Don continued his tirade, which ended with, "I seldom get sick, and even if I do, I always come to work."

When the others left, I asked Don if he only opened his mouth to change feet. I reminded him that both of the men he had been talking to had recently been off with this same flu. He looked embarrassed, said he'd forgotten, and went in to the other office to apologize, saying, "You know I didn't mean you. I was talking about all of those other fakers."

The next morning Don walked into the office with the same flu, and ended up being off work for several days. I couldn't help myself. I laughed and told Don that what he didn't understand, the Spooks would make him wear so he could see how those "faking employees" felt. They put him in the other man's shoes for a while to learn a little empathy and compassion. I laughed at him every time he walked in sneezing and blowing, looking and feeling absolutely miserable.

It was a good lesson in attitude and the Law of Return for Don, but I shouldn't have enjoyed the lesson so much. Guess who came down with the virus three days later? That's right, good old self-righteous me.

And I seldom ever get any of the viral flus that are so contagious. Guess the Spooks thought I could use a lesson in empathy and attitude too. Don thought the whole lesson was just great, especially when he got the last laugh, but I never heard him rave about those lazy weaklings who get sick all the time after that. We both learned.

## *When to Examine Your Behavior*

When something happens in your life that seems unfair or unjust, examine your own behavior. Look for any incident in your past where you may have been responsible for similar actions. You'll be surprised how often your memory will supply you with vivid details you'd rather forget.

The most important thing to remember is to try to be honest with yourself, learn from the experience, and sincerely try not to make the same mistake again. We all wish we could have the chance to undo something we're sorry for, and we hear, "If I only had my life to live over again, I would do things differently." You don't have to wait to be different; you can start today.

Don't worry; the Spooks will give you the chance to prove you have learned, and they always do. Just recognize the opportunity when it comes to you, and look for the Law of Return in action around you.

---

**PSYCHIC TIP: SEE THE LAW OF RETURN IN YOUR LIFE**

You're able to see the Law of Return most quickly when it happens to others. It is easy to see another's mistakes and how that person "got what was coming." It's also easy to be the judge and jury. But just remember, nothing ever happens in your life that you haven't earned—good or bad—either in this lifetime through the Law of Return or as karma from a previous existence. Instead of saying "Why me?" or "Poor me," sincerely look at your own behavior to truly discover what you did to be presented with this learning experience. Solve the mystery, learn from your mistakes, and remember: When everything seems hardest your soul is learning the most.

Our entire lifetime is like a very interesting puzzle. Try to learn something new each day or solve some of the unexpected things presented to you, and remember you will always be given another chance.

# CHAPTER FOUR

# Death and Dying

It is kind of an in-house joke that every time I get sick, I look around real fast for my dad. If I can't find him, then I know I'm going to survive, whether I want to or not.

My father really didn't know if he believed in any of this psychic nonsense or not. He was very intelligent, having graduated from a military college at the ripe old age of eighteen to serve in World War I. He was raised a Catholic, didn't really go to any church, but believed very strongly in a power greater than we are. He humored my mother and the rest of us in our beliefs until just before his death, when he started having, as he put it, "the damnedest dreams."

Dad died very slowly from cancer. He was ill for seven years before a real diagnosis was made. He admitted he had known it was terminal for over a year before his death, wasn't surprised, and he had been getting his affairs in order. We discovered after his death that this included writing letters to people who had been his friends and business associates telling them how much he appreciated knowing them, and that he would be gone by the time they received the letter. Quite a legacy for the rest of us to live up to! He was a very logical, practical, no-nonsense type of person, which is one reason the events surrounding his death were so unusual.

Rockie and I had moved in with my parents the last three weeks of my father's life to help Mom in caring for him. We kept Dad at home at his request. Mom, who was a little senile and extremely tired, was convinced that all those pain pills weren't good for Dad, so she just wouldn't give them to him if we weren't there to insist. It wasn't practical to drive across town four to six times a day to medicate Dad and keep the pain under control. Besides, both parents needed help at night. Dad was in a semi-conscious state a lot of the time, slept a lot, but was able by sheer will power to pull himself up from a semi-coma, walk into the next room and hold intelligent, logical conversations with whoever had come to visit. He had a very keen mind and his memory and mental faculties were fully intact right to the end.

Just seven days before his death, he pulled himself up from this near-coma state to talk to our youngest son on the phone. Mark had joined the Navy and was in boot camp in San Diego. He had obtained special permission to call his dying grandfather. They visited for about five minutes, during which Dad said goodbye to Mark, thanked him for various happy memories, and wished him luck. This was from a man who was too sick to eat and too weak to sit up alone.

## *Dreams Prepare the Dying*

During the last two months, Dad would come out to the living room and visit with us, eat if possible, and occasionally tell us about one of these "damnedest dreams." He said they all seemed to be so real, but the most puzzling thing to Dad was that most of them were associated with people whom he knew were already dead. This included his cousin, aunt, father, friends he knew were dead, and my brother Dick, who had died twenty years before. This just didn't seem logical to him.

One dream I distinctly remember him telling me involved his cousin Charlie. In Dad's dream, he was visiting Charlie and his aunt. They lived in a beautiful rock home on an island in the middle of a crystal-clear lake. Charlie had been bragging to Dad about how good the fishing was, and they had eaten a fantastic fish dinner Dad's aunt had cooked. Dad decided he would have to leave. They told him not to worry, he'd be back "real soon" and they had a cabin already outfitted for him to live in when he returned. He replied that he thought it was a wonderful offer and would consider it, but right now he had to get back to the family. Dad couldn't get over how really beautiful the location had been, the vibrant colors, the perfection.

On one occasion, Dad woke us, shouting, at three o'clock in the morning. We leaped out of bed, thinking Dad was in terrible pain or was dying at that moment. Much to my surprise, when I got to his room, he was sitting up in bed. Dad was doing something with his hands on the bedspread and shouting "Dick," my dead brother's name, over and over. I watched for a minute, decided it must be some kind of dream or nightmare, and gently woke my father. He awoke laughing and said, "Oh, it's just you. I was having the damnedest dream. I was with Dick and we were drinking whiskey, playing poker, and splitting up the territory!" Neither of them were drinkers during their lives, only having a drink on special occasions, so I could assume this was indeed a special occasion. The only card game Dick ever played was poker, as he would never get involved in the marathon pinochle games Dad used to organize in the family, and I'd never seen my father play poker at home. Splitting up the territory? Not exactly what I thought souls did on the other side, but who knows? This left us with some different ideas about what might be possible on the astral plane, and it sounds like a lot more fun than angelically flapping your wings.

Five days before his death, my father got to the point where he had lost the swallow reflex and we were no longer able to give him pain medication orally. It was my task to explain the situation to Dad and convince him it was time to go to the hospital. I was only able to convince Dad by agreeing to go with him and staying as long as he needed me. While waiting for the ambulance, he said, "Well, I guess it's time to cash in my chips. I've had a good life. I've done pretty much what I wanted and needed to do, and I'm ready to go." We talked about caring for my mother, and then about his strange dreams. He told me he knew now that they weren't just dreams and that he had been actually seeing people who were dead. He couldn't explain how it was possible and it didn't really fit in with his life-long beliefs. He knew he had been really seeing Dick, and that his cousin, father, and a lot of friends were waiting for him. I was sitting there with tears rolling down my cheeks and I said, "Well, you know Dick will be there to meet you for sure." My father then said, "I know that. There's one thing I want you to know. When it's your time to go, I'll come for you."

I went with my father to the hospital and stayed all of the first night. He only awoke one time. He sat up in bed, and told me how beautiful his dream was, and how happy he was. I asked if he was having any pain now and if he felt OK about being in the hospital. He said he was fine and I should go home. I stayed the rest of that night as promised and he never came out of the coma again or spoke to anyone else. The doctors said it was only the pain that had kept awakening him and that as soon as the morphine had taken affect, he had dropped into a deep coma.

We visited repeatedly, but he was always unresponsive. I told the nurses that my father would die on Wednesday and I wanted them to be sure to call me or my husband, not my mother.

That way we would be able to be with her when she got the news. The head nurse said, "Oh, he's not that bad yet. It could be a long time." Dad died on Wednesday just as the Spooks had said, and that nurse later came to me for readings and was with my mother the morning she died.

In some way no one can understand, Dad sent a message to Rockie at work just before his death. Rockie suddenly got the overwhelming urge to leave work one hour early and go directly to the hospital. He walked in just as Dad took his last breath and was with him for the last couple of minutes. I believe this was more to comfort the rest of the family regarding what happened at the moment of death than because Dad needed someone there. He never regained consciousness; he just left. Even though Rockie was a son-in-law, he was the only one my father trusted for his physical needs at the end. He said, "Rockie would understand. He has been very sick and he knows how it feels." I'm sure there was a very strong karmic tie between the two of them and Dad will be there for Rockie also.

## *My Psychic Roots*

Of course, when we went home to tell Mom, she already knew, but then she always did. I was just five when my mother's father died. When they delivered the message to our home in the middle of the night, the shopkeeper didn't know how to tell her. She just saved him the trouble by saying, "I know. My father died from pneumonia at three o'clock this afternoon. He already came to say goodbye." There was no logical way she could have known. He was healthy, well, and lived in Minnesota. We lived in California, with no phone. My grandfather had caught pneumonia five days earlier at the age of seventy-three when he had insisted on riding his bicycle to work in a snow storm. He still worked full time as a machinist and was a tough, little old German man.

My mother was very psychic, and read cards (with the same system I use), tea leaves, and palms. She had precognitive dreams that came true and in general scared the hell out of me as a kid! Our concern about breaking the news to Mom was that we weren't sure of her mental state at the time. She had been caring for a very sick man for a long time and was very tired. We shouldn't have worried. She said, "Now don't grieve too much or you will retard your dad's progress." This was the same advice she had given my sister-in-law and the rest of us when my brother Dick had died years before, and he had been her favorite son. She believed the soul needed to move on and upward as soon as the body died, and excessive grieving would keep the soul around on the earth to help those left behind.

Mom was sad that she wouldn't get to see Dad anymore, but didn't doubt for one moment that she was still able to communicate with him. We found her in his closet the next day giving him the dickens because she couldn't find his good dress suit for the funeral. She was saying, "Not the green pants and orange sweatshirt, Al. It's just not proper. Now where did you hide the suit?" The suit turned up in the back of the guest closet out in the hall, the only item of Dad's clothing in there. She was firmly convinced he hid the suit, either before or after his death.

The green pants and the orange sweatshirt (an awful combination) were my father's favorite work clothes for around the house. He had been required to wear suits and ties for work most of his life and really hated to dress up after he retired.

While the funeral arrangements were in progress, our oldest son, Rockie Jr., was involved in a peculiar incident. He went to a local drive-in restaurant and ordered milkshakes and hamburgers to go for himself and his future bride. When the carhop delivered the food it wasn't packaged to go. Rockie insisted he had placed the order that way and she continued to argue. He finally said, "Why would I order for two, when I'm all alone?" The waitress got quite angry and said, "What do you mean, alone? Where's the old guy with the green pants and the orange sweatshirt who was with you when you came in?" Rockie started laughing when he realized she had just seen his dead grandfather, but there was no way he could explain that to her. He had felt his grandfather's presence and was thinking of him when he drove up to order, but hadn't seen him. By some unknown ability, the waitress had. Rockie's impression was that Grandpa thought it was pretty funny too, but the waitress was very angry. My dad had always enjoyed our son's sense of humor and apparently had chosen to remind him in this way.

Dad continued to make his presence felt with various members of the family during the following days, to the point where I'm sure the funeral director thought we were the weirdest family he had ever had to deal with. As the hearse led the procession into the cemetery, everyone in the lead family car looked at each other and simultaneously started laughing. We had all felt Dad's very alive sense of humor and heard him tell the same joke.

The cemetery was very modern, with no vertical tombstones, and it really resembled a golf course. Dad had enjoyed playing golf and could tell a joke better than anyone we knew. One of his favorite stories was the joke we all heard. It seems there were two guys out playing golf on a Saturday afternoon. Just then a funeral procession passed on the street and one of the golfers stopped, removed his hat, and bowed his head. The other golfer said, "Gee, that was a very respectful, considerate gesture" To which the other golfer replied, "It was the only decent thing to do. After all, we would have been married forty-five years next Saturday."

## *Dad Communicates from the Other Side*

Dad continued to contact us in various ways in the following months. One night, about a month after his death, I awoke from a sound sleep to hear his voice very clearly in our room saying, "This is God's country, this is really God's country." Then about three months later, I went to see my psychic and teacher to ask if my father was happy. She replied, "Happy isn't the word. Satisfied, content, is better. Oh, he has a message for you. He says he hasn't forgotten, and when it's your time to go, he will come for you." I nearly fell off of the chair, because there was no way she should have been able to quote my father, word for word. I hadn't told anyone other than Rockie at that time. She then went on to say that there was something Dad wanted us to have. It was in a black box and we needed to look for it. We looked and found the box. Inside was a letter from my father, written before his death, thanking us for helping him and for caring for Mom after his death.

If we hadn't been believers before, we certainly would have been after receiving this message from beyond the grave, especially from a self-professed doubter.

About six months later, Rockie and I arranged to take my mother to Hawaii, which had been a lifelong dream of my father's. Any possibility of taking the trip had become more remote as Dad's health gradually dwindled away. We had sold our house and moved in with Mom to care for her two weeks after my father died. It became increasingly obvious that she couldn't be left alone.

My mother was a tiny little lady, with silver hair and twinkling blue eyes. She was still very pretty at seventy-one years of age. She could be mentally with us 100 percent one minute and then get confused or strange the next. It was 1974, and she was perfectly capable of saying things that shocked people at that time. She really enjoyed the flight on the 747 to Hawaii, even though she had feared flying all of her life. We were not sure what her reaction would be and feared a last-minute cancellation. On the flight over, she stuck her head in the first-class section and decided that was the way she wanted to fly home.

When we arrived in Hawaii, we stopped at the ticket counter to have our tickets changed to first class for the return trip. When she found out how much the difference in fare would be, she said, "I just wanted to fly first class, not buy the damn plane." She stomped off, refusing to pay the difference even when we offered to make it our treat. This reaction would have been much more typical of my Scottish father, and we laughed, thinking how Dad was still with us.

Mom told various people we met that she was on this trip because she and Dad hadn't been able to make it together, but he was with us in spirit. One of the bands on the Kona Coast kind of adopted Mom and played the old songs she and Dad would have wanted to hear. She was having a ball.

We had reservations at the Polynesian Cultural Center for a show one night and decided to try to make it very special for Mom. We had tried to order an orchid lei for her, but had been told that we would have to drive back to Honolulu to get one, because they didn't have any access to orchids. We were disappointed; orchids had always been the flowers my dad had given Mom, even on their golden wedding anniversary. The people who ran the motel said they could make a fresh plumera lei for her from the trees that grew around the area, so we settled for that.

The whole evening was great, but as we started walking back to our motel a strong, very cool wind came up. Rockie and I tucked Mom in between us and decided to take a back road to the motel which would be much faster, though less scenic, and would provide some protection from the wind. This was the back road where all of the tour buses were parked. As we hurried along, we saw something ahead of us lying on the ground, sparkling in the moonlight. We were all curious, because it almost glowed. When we reached the spot, Rockie stooped down, picked the object up and handed it to my mother. She was thrilled, and kept saying, "It's from Dad. Oh, thank you, Al. I just knew you were with us." It was a perfect lavender orchid lei. Not crushed, as if it had been discarded or dropped accidentally, but absolutely perfect, as if it had just been delivered from a florist shop. It sparkled because of the little drops of dew on the petals. Mom knew my dad had sent it to her, was still with her, and loved her.

We have pictures of her wearing the orchid lei under a palm tree in Hawaii. I don't know how he did it, or what set of coincidences were set in motion to make that particular lei show up in exactly that spot on that night, but I know my dad sent orchids to Mom six months after his death.

## *Mom's Journey Home*

Which brings us to the second part of this particular story. As mentioned, my mother was very psychic, while Dad didn't understand or believe any of that "hooey." Mom only did readings for family or close friends and was a little afraid of her abilities. She had been raised as a good Catholic child in a large Polish/German family, attended Catholic school, and was a little uncomfortable with the whole psychic realm. She had shown me a little about reading palms when I was very small, and I can remember reading palms in elementary school for friends until a very concerned teacher told me that what I was doing was evil, the devil's work.

Attitudes toward psychic beliefs in that time were considerably different than they are today. Most thought of psychics as evil, and since Mom didn't want to be avoided by other people, she just buried her abilities. They would surface as they did when her father died or when she did readings for my older sister's friends during World War II. After one altogether too-accurate reading for myself, I decided I wouldn't ever let Mom read for me again. It was always bad news and I'd just as soon not know. Besides, knowing how to read palms had just gotten me into trouble in school, so I decided to avoid the whole thing for the rest of my life. Ha!

We could all recall times when Mom just knew things in advance. It was difficult being raised by someone who could read your mind. I remember her teasingly asking my brother Dick why he was getting so dressed up for a date. She said, "What are you doing? Running away to Yuma to get married?" That is exactly what he was doing, and he almost confessed when she said that.

In October 1951, my parents were at home when both of them heard someone calling "Mrs. Rose" (my mother's name) over and over. They both went outside to investigate and couldn't see anyone near their home, which was on three acres out in the country. Mom immediately started thinking of and praying for my older brother, Dick, who was in Korea at the time. When we got home that night, she told us to pray also, but she didn't know why it must be for Dick, just that he needed help from all of us right then.

About three days later, they got the news that Dick had been very badly injured by an artillery shell at exactly the time they heard the voice calling. His injuries were so serious that he was given the last rites in the field and again at the hospital. He survived and lived for seven more years before dying as a result of the injuries.

They both heard the voice calling, but only Mom understood what it meant. Both of my parents had a very strict religious upbringing but, by this time, Mom could see no conflict between God and the psychic events in her life. As far as she was concerned, if God didn't want her to know these things so she could help others, the gift would be taken away from her. I have finally come to the same conclusion.

After Dad died, we lived with Mom for the next two and one-half years, during which time she alternately taught us or drove us nuts, depending on her mental state. She had lost all concept of time and was perfectly capable of having a lamb roast prepared for dinner at noon, then giving us the devil at five when we got home from work for being so inconsiderate to be late for dinner. Another time, she decided to make homemade soup out of extra crispy fried chicken left over from the previous night. Do you have any idea what "Extra Crispy" batter turns into after being boiled with vegetables and a can of fruit cocktail for five hours? Believe me, you don't want to know!

On the other hand, she showed us some of her amazing abilities, including her skill in turning off pain at will.

When Dad was in the hospital, Mom tripped on a rug in the waiting room, said she was just fine, and walked on a broken foot for the next four hours. Another time she broke her arm in the middle of the night, didn't say a word to anyone, and just went back to sleep. We didn't know she had even fallen until the next morning when she got up with a swollen, black and blue arm. She insisted it really didn't hurt and we had to argue to get her to go to the doctor.

When Mom was seventy-two years old, she decided one afternoon that she would die when she was seventy-three. According to her logic, her father and husband had both died at seventy-three, and quite a few of her friends had left at that age. Since this was only a few months before her seventy-third birthday, we tried to convince her this was just foolishness. She was healthy, happy, and had a lot to live for. Mom turned seventy-three in December, they found she had terminal bowel cancer the middle of February, and she died the fourth of April. Just as she had predicted. Oddly enough, my mother and father had each lived almost the exact number of years, months, and days in this lifetime. They had died from the same disease, in the same hospital, and with the same doctor.

Once again, we kept Mom at home until the last possible moment, with home nursing help as needed. Our daughter was living with us at the time and she helped care for Mom right to the end. This helped to encourage her in her decision to work in the nursing field. We all believe everyone should be allowed to die with respect and dignity, surrounded by those they love. You cannot have that dignity if the body is experiencing terrible pain. The proper medications should be given to ease the discomfort during this period.

Mom had been hospitalized for surgery for a short time in February and had managed to baffle the medical profession with her ability to ignore pain. The doctors said the surgery she had undergone was one of the most painful types, yet she had never asked for pain medication and they had administered it at times mainly because they couldn't believe she was comfortable. She was totally unconcerned with the fact that she was dying and just didn't want to discuss it. If she did it was only to talk about joining Dad and other friends and relatives. Perhaps if she hadn't gotten so senile by that time, she might have been able to tell us a lot more.

We had to hospitalize Mom the night before she died, because she was unable to swallow the nausea medication and was so deathly sick. When the ambulance drivers came to pick her up, she was twinkle-eyed and happy. She kept telling them she was going to Hawaii with her husband. They exchanged looks, firmly convinced Mom was just out of her mind. When she got to the hospital, she did the same thing with the nursing staff and doctors. We knew what she meant and didn't doubt for one minute that she was joining Dad in Hawaii. When admitted, Mom had almost no pulse or blood pressure, and she was in critical condition. Three hours later her doctor called, quite upset because we had admitted her. Apparently she was so happy and animated, she had once again taken control of her bodily functions to the point she was again confusing the medical profession. We tried to explain to the doctor that Mom was dying, very soon, probably within hours and was capable of this control. Have you ever tried to tell a doctor his patient is dying? Forget it! His response was that he intended to release her in the morning.

The next morning the hospital called at seven and said Mom was dying and we'd better hurry if we wanted to say goodbye. When we arrived Mom was smiling and happy, but she was unable to talk since her lungs were so congested. Even so, she kept pointing to one area of the ceiling and tapping our arms. She wanted us to see what she was seeing. We asked her who was on the reception committee, and she responded to various names by nodding or shaking her head. At times she would seem to look around for someone, find them in the group, be very pleased or surprised, and then try to get us to see. We asked if she and Dad were going to Hawaii right away—she only nodded again, very happily. She also let us know she wanted the last rites of the Catholic Church. When the priest finished and anointed her head, she closed her eyes and her spirit just left. My sister and her husband were with us and we all had the distinct sensation that Mom just shot into the arms of those waiting at the moment of her death. The next instant they all zoomed away and we were left with a strange feeling of loneliness. The sensation was as if she and the group who had come for her had just left in a 747 and we were left in the backwash, trying to understand.

None of us were able to see what she was seeing. I wish we could have. We just knew she was extremely happy and anxious to go, and maybe a little frustrated because we were all so blind. We know Mom and Dad left for Hawaii in that instant. I wonder if anyone on the Big Island noticed the couple waltzing so beautifully that April morning? I'm sure they would have noted the beautiful lavender orchid lei the tiny little lady was wearing! I never spoke to my mother's doctor after the last conversation the night before her death. He wouldn't have been able to understand how we knew her death was so close when, in his medical judgment, it just wasn't possible. I believe when Mom chose to go, she just did so through her ability to control her body. From what I've heard and read, the ancient ones from Indian tribes were able to do this same thing, just sit under a tree and will their spirit to leave, and it did.

During her lifetime, my mother never feared death and I believe this came from her true understanding of life and death, and her faith in what she believed. She was the one comforting and calming other members of the family when her son Dick died when he was only twenty-eight. She knew when people died they just left the body like a very worn, old set of clothes. (Maybe like the green pants and the orange shirt that belonged to my father.) She also knew living was the problem, not dying.

Several months after Mom's funeral I had a very funny dream about her. It was so like her, I didn't need Rockie to help me interpret. In the dream, I was in the church waiting for the funeral to begin and Mom wouldn't behave herself. She kept climbing out of the coffin and sitting on the edge. I kept trying to explain why she had to lie down and behave in a proper dead fashion. She said, "But I'm not dead. You know I'm not dead and I know I'm not dead, so why do I have to pretend that I am?" To this I replied, "I know you aren't dead, but everyone else thinks you are, and if you don't act right you'll scare them. Now, get back in there, lie down with your arms crossed, and quit twinkling your eyes and grinning at everyone." She said she intended to jump right out of that box as soon as we all left and quit pretending just because people said she should. At this, she assumed the right position, winked at me, smiled, and said, "Like this, Mommy?" just like a sassy little child.

I know this was Mom's way of making contact to let us know she was alive and well on the other side, just as feisty as ever and doing her own thing.

## *Your Loved Ones Are Still Speaking to You*

The fear of death and the unknown drives people to do irrational things throughout their lives. It is the one fear and concern we all have. Researchers have found that small children seem better able to deal with terminal illness than the adults who surround them. Perhaps it is because they are still close enough to the astral plane to remember. Quite often, my readings will be involved in helping someone understand death, especially when they have just lost a loved one.

One really evolved soul I read for in Texas was trying to stay with her father as much as possible after he had open-heart surgery. She wanted to be with him during the transition if he was not able to survive the trauma of the surgery. He was eighty-four years old and the Spooks had advised that this would be too much for him and he would choose to leave. He appeared to be coming through the surgery satisfactorily and by the eighth day the daughter was exhausted. She left his side just long enough to run a couple of errands and return to her apartment for a few minutes. She arrived just in time to get the call from the hospital saying that her father had died. This was totally unexpected by his medical team.

I explained to her that sometimes the actual moment of death is something a soul chooses to do in private. Perhaps she would have had difficulty in letting him go. Some souls apparently feel that privacy is needed at the moment of death, just as a person prefers privacy when going to the bathroom. Some things you really want to do alone.

I have used this notion to explain to some of my clients why their loved one left during just those few minutes. This is a choice the individual soul makes. My mother allowed us to be with her, probably so we could help explain dying to others.

This same lady in Texas now finds change lying on the ground in front of her whenever her father wants to contact her. She knows it is from him, and he is just saying hello and thank you to her. She is caring for her elderly mother and doing a fantastic job. Her father arranged for her to find thirty-five dollars the day before her birthday. The Spooks said he wanted her to buy something pink for herself. I don't know how souls who have made the transition are able to manipulate things in this physical world, but they do.

On his birthday, two years after his death, he arranged to have the drawer on his old desk fall out, revealing the place he had hidden two cards she had sent to him for his birthdays before he died. He just wanted her to remember him and also to know how much her thoughtfulness had meant to him in the past and that he had kept the cards in appreciation.

Another client of mine also finds change in her pathway and once received orchids from her father. She had accidentally driven to the cemetery where he is buried when she was concentrating on a particularly vexing problem. When she realized she was just outside the gates, she decided to run in and say "Hi" to her dad. She turned to leave the graveside and found a large bouquet of orchids in the path between where she stood and the gateway. She said the bouquet was so large it would have cost a small fortune. She says she knew they were not there when she came in, or she would have tripped over them. She walked around the orchids, but told her dad, "Thank you. They are beautiful." I guess the men on the other side are partial to orchids. He is definitely helping to increase her law practice and has helped her make some very important changes in her life since his death. Sometimes our parents can help us and teach us more after they have left the earthly plane.

## Watch for Messages Through Others

One afternoon I was in the nearby airport waiting for my husband to arrive when I noticed a young girl and an elderly man enter. They talked quietly for a few minutes, shook hands, and the man left. The girl sat in a chair across the waiting room from me, and I went back to reading my book. For some unknown reason I kept checking on her and then noticed she had tears silently running down her cheeks. At that moment, the Spooks said, "Go talk to her." Consciously, I thought "No way. What would I say? It's her business, so leave her alone." The thought persisted, but I wasn't about to walk up to a total stranger who would probably believe I was some kind of a nut, and make a fool of myself. This went on for about half an hour.

Finally, I went to the restroom to "hide out," but I couldn't get away from my nagging Spooks. Then suddenly I knew who was trying to contact her, and I knew the message. I hurried back out to tell her what I was receiving, but she was already in the sealed-off boarding area. I walked over to the area where my husband was to disembark, feeling I had really failed my Spooks, when suddenly the girl walked by within an arm's length of where I was standing. I gave her the message. It was, "Don't grieve. I'm still with you and will be whenever you need me." I told her it was from the woman who had just died. Then I asked her if it was her mother or grandmother. The girl looked at me strangely and then started laughing and crying at the same time.

She told me she had just come from her grandmother's funeral. She had found the grandmother only a few years before; the family had been split up when she was very young. She felt so cheated, because she really loved this long-lost grandmother and felt she needed her in this life. She asked how I knew and if I was "some kind of a psychic or something." I admitted it and apologized for intercepting her, and briefly explained that I never read for anyone unless they asked. In this case, the grandmother's need to get a message to her was so strong, I couldn't ignore it. Then I gave her the next part of the message, which was that she was pregnant and would have a healthy girl in six months. She admitted that she was expecting, no one knew except her doctor, and she was three months along. She was very pleased and relieved by the message. We talked for a few more minutes, then her flight was called for the last time. We didn't even exchange names, but she boarded the plane smiling and waving. She just knew her grandmother really was still alive in mind and soul, and still available for her.

Even though I usually don't do these strange things, I felt this was one of the exceptions. Besides, the Spooks gave me one more chance after I thought I had blown it, so I had to respond. Somewhere on the East Coast, a young woman has probably told friends about this strange airport encounter. I hope that the message from the other side helped her to overcome her grief and feelings of loss. Maybe she has gone on to learn more about parapsychology and, who knows, maybe her grandmother helps her when she needs someone.

## *Watch for Jokes, Too*

The departed often have a great sense of humor. A friend of mine told me of a crazy situation that occurred in his family when his mother-in-law died. Apparently, she was at home with them and he awakened very startled at two in the morning, knowing his wife's mother had died in the next bedroom. After he had verified the fact, he called the local funeral home, and was told they would be out in thirty minutes. There were two families with the same last name on that street and the funeral director picked the other family by mistake. He went to the door and told the sleepy elderly gentleman who answered that he was from the funeral home to pick up Mrs. Martin. The poor old man yawned, scratched his head, and said "Well, she's in the bedroom, but I thought she was just sleeping. Just a minute, let me go check."

After he got over his embarrassment and apologized, the funeral director and my friend stood on the front porch laughing quietly about the incident, then feeling guilty because of the laughter. They shouldn't have felt guilty. It is entirely possible his mother-in-law orchestrated the whole episode. She had never gotten along with the other Mrs. Martin, and may very well have set up the whole scene as a "Gotcha, one last time" on the other Mrs. Martin. She was probably enjoying it more than they were!

Since I first started writing this book, my sister and her husband, who were our very good friends besides being related, have both died. If I know them, they have found out how to play golf all day and dance all night in the astral plane. They died within nine months of each other; the Spooks say when two souls are very close, with their karma entwined, they usually leave as close together as possible, usually within two years. One of them really doesn't have much left to learn or do without a soul mate.

My oldest brother has also died from prostate cancer. I gave him static about going to join our folks, our sister and her husband, and our brother Dick and his wife. I know they were planning a family reunion and not inviting us younger kids. Same old story, the younger kids always get left out and have to wait their turn. Oh well, I know there will even be more people on my reception committee. After my tirade, my brother said, "When it's your time, we'll have a special party just for you, so quit being such a brat!" That was probably the last thing he ever said to me before he died. It does feel kind of strange when you have more of your family on the other side than on this one. I can sympathize with those individuals who live to be so old that all of their friends and relatives are gone.

## *Death Is Really Just the Finish Line*

Most of us feel such a great loss when people we care for die, partly because we miss them, and partly due to fear of the unknown. If we could only realize that when a person dies on this earth, they are immediately home in the astral plane where they came from originally. Just realize that the person finished the goals set for this lifetime, even though it might have been very short, and went home.

I often feel we really have the entire emotional field backward when it comes to funerals and births. We should rejoice at a funeral because that soul just graduated. If we must mourn or be thoughtful, it should be at a birth of a new baby, as that soul has just returned to do it all over again. In truth, we should be happy at the birth also, because that little soul may have been waiting a long time for the right set of circumstances to return to further its education.

We have all been taught that it is disrespectful to the dead if we get caught laughing or being happy when someone close to us dies. The Spooks say that is a societal taboo and has nothing to do with the attitude or feelings in the astral plane. I personally want everyone laughing, being happy, and having one great party at my funeral, because I can guarantee you I certainly won't be mourning when my soul finishes and gets to go home. I've also threatened to come back and "haunt" anyone who isn't enjoying themselves!

## *Leave a Legacy for the Living*

My brother talked openly and seriously, or foolishly, about his impending death, which I think is really important. When I think of leaving a legacy that will be hard to follow, well, my brother outdid even my dad. He was on the hospice program and took care of all the details involved in dying, even picking his own funeral arrangements and music. He did everything humanly possible to make things easier on his wife, including rearranging all of their finances, housing, etc., to make her more comfortable and safe. Since I will probably leave out some of the most important details, even if I know when I am going to die, I'll just have to ask my Spooks for some help.

With my perverted sense of humor, I plan to enjoy myself when I go home. I don't want to feel guilty because I'm happy and everyone I've left behind is feeling sad. This is a journey we all have to make, and we usually make it alone. We come alone and we leave alone, and each of us "alone" is responsible for our own behavior. Don't try to interpret that to mean that you shouldn't help others to reach their goals; you should. Just don't judge them until you have "walked a mile in their moccasins."

As I said in the beginning of this chapter, I know Dad will be there when it's my time to go. So will my brothers and maybe my sister, unless she's off on a trip of some sort. There are so many souls that we are close to on the other side that weren't even alive during our current lifetime. I have no fear of death and never have, but I joke about looking around for my dad. In truth, the things our parents taught us when they left this world gave every member of the family a different attitude about death and dying. We're kind of looking forward to the big family reunion on the astral plane, but I don't know about "drinking whiskey and splitting up the territory." Guess I'll just have to wait and see.

## *Recognize Communication from the Other Side*

I get a heads up and a "Hi" from some of my family on the other side all the time. Just recently I was doing a reading for a young woman for the first time. Suddenly I said, "You have a message for me." She denied it and we continued to talk. Then she told me how honored she had been to be allowed to be with her uncle when he died the month before. I asked her what had happened. She said she was in his hospital room while he was dying and, in an effort to ease the transition for him, she said, "It's OK, Uncle Al. Aunt Rose is here for you. She will help you make the transition. Just let go and go toward the light with her." This totally surprised me and I asked her to repeat it to make sure I was hearing it right. My father and my brother, who are both on the other side, were named Al Rose. It was a "Hi" from both of them. It still surprises me when this happens because it is by the deceased person's choice, not mine, and my father has been gone for nearly thirty-two years. Obviously time has nothing to do with loving or caring.

Please remember that when someone you loved dies, they are just going to another plane or dimension. The physical body dies, but the soul never does. They still care for you, they remember the love and things you have shared, and they will be waiting on the other side for you when you finish your current lesson.

Keep your eyes and ears open for the gentle messages your loved ones send from the other side. Sometimes they will be as obvious as my dad's written message after his death or as subtle as the coins found by a couple of my clients that they recognize as coming from their fathers. This is probably part of a special memory of a shared treat with their fathers or maybe just the weekly allowance, but special for them and a gift from him.

It can be an object that is out of place, but relates to some secret you may have shared, even to a book turned upside down in the bookcase when the title is significant to a memory of that person. Listen to songs being played that strike a memory. My Dad's favorite tune was "Claire de Lune." When my daughter gave me a music box for Christmas with that song, I cried because I knew Dad was also involved. It was a Merry Christmas from him also, because he got her to pick that tune.

I have been told that a person is never dead as long as someone who is alive remembers them. Say "Hi, I love you," and continue to remember, because they haven't forgotten you!

---

### PSYCHIC TIP: COMMUNICATE WITH LOVED ONES ON THE ASTRAL PLANE

Pay attention to the little insignificant things that bring back a memory of a special person who is on the other side. Some of the things I have seen and heard about are:

- A flower someone liked or that makes you think of her.
- A special fragrance, perfume, cologne, or even a tobacco smell, like a pipe.
- An odor that was associated with someone, maybe not so nice.
- A sunset or sunrise that jogs your memory of one shared long ago.
- Catching a glimpse of someone in the distance who looks just like the person. When you get close, it isn't, but it certainly made you remember for a moment.
- Friends or family reminiscing about some event or memory.
- Coming across a memento you forgot or didn't know you had. (I recently found the top decoration from my parents' fiftieth wedding anniversary cake. I didn't know it was packed in an old box when my mother died in 1976.)
- Driving in a location that brings back memories.
- Seeing a television show or personality the person on the other side loved or hated.
- Renting an old movie that you and that person saw together years ago.

Another method: Just before going to sleep, say, "I am going to see [name] tonight." Say it three times, and try to remember your dream. It can be unbelievably real! Remember, the person is on the astral plane, which is just where you are going when you fall asleep. Just remind yourself to look that person up. Repeating the above three times is like knocking on the door!

When you wake up, write down what you remember. If you are serious about remembering, the Spooks will help you remember more.

Last, listen for the voice behind your right shoulder. It is not your imagination!

# CHAPTER FIVE

# Out-of-Body Experiences and Free Will

We have all started falling asleep, only to suddenly jump and be startled into full wakefulness. Sometimes this is accompanied by a partial dream of falling or being chased, or sometimes just a relaxed, dozing feeling. My Spooks say this is a physical response natural to the human body when your soul or "astral self" is just starting to leave for the night and something frightens or disturbs you. You are going home, returning to the astral plane for rejuvenation, help with problems, and answers to situations that are troubling you. When you are disturbed by some outside distraction, noise, or fear, you automatically "jump" back into your body.

We never fully disconnect from our body while it is living. Instead, it remains connected by a silver cord—no matter how far we travel in the astral world. When you return suddenly, it results in the cord being snapped like a rubber band and the startled, fearful feeling is normal. It is the normal adrenalin rush; it's just disturbing.

In Ecclesiastes 12:6, the Bible mentions the "Golden Bowl" and "Silver Cord" being loosed or broken. This is basically the aura and the cord connecting our physical bodies to our astral body or soul. Then, in verse 7, it says, "Then shall the dust return to Earth and the spirit shall return unto God who gave it." The physical body returns to the earth, and the astral body or soul returns to the astral plane (or "heaven," if you prefer).

In many of the paintings from the old masters, individuals such as Christ, angels, and others of high spiritual rank are shown with a very obvious halo, the "Golden Bowl." This is really the soul radiating from the body.

Some psychics are able to see the aura very clearly. My youngest son is able to see the aura and all of its colors (more on auras in chapter 8). The main point is that the aura shows the presence of the energy force, which is resident in every person, tree, plant, and living thing. Even rocks, especially crystals, have an aura of their own. You can now see, with special photography, the aura or electrical force emanating from a body. Some scientists are very close to being able to prove the physical evidence of the presence of a soul, or your astral self.

## The Astral Plane: A Refresher

As a refresher, let's take a look once more at the nature of the astral plane.

The astral plane is the plane just above the earth. According to the Spooks, others beyond the astral plane include the plane of enlightenment, the plane of light, and many more.

As your soul progresses, it moves from one plane to the next. These are areas inhabited by souls at differing levels of knowledge and growth. Since we are the youngest souls, we are still only moving back and forth from the astral plane, our home base, to the earth for our education. While our ultimate goal is to return to our source of origin and become part of God, our goal at present is just to complete this particular earth cycle and gain as much knowledge as possible during this lifetime. Eventually, we'll "graduate" out of the astral plane to the next level of awareness.

## The Astral Plane: Work Zone

When you astrally project or when your soul leaves the body, the cord remains connected and enough of the energy force is left to watch over and protect the sleeping physical body. If any harm is about to happen, the soul becomes aware and your Spooks snap you back into full awareness with a rush of adrenaline or the "fight or flight syndrome." Your Spooks want to protect your body as much as you do. Your body may not be in harm's way, but some small noise or insignificant action makes you want to come back to check. For instance, when you snap back into wakefulness, someone may have just entered your room and you return to find out why.

If your astral self returns to the physical body and is not aligned correctly, as sometimes happens when your sleep is disturbed, you can wake with a disoriented feeling, a headache, or dizziness. Usually, if you are able to go back to sleep for a short period of time, this feeling will leave. This gives your soul and physical body an opportunity to realign.

Why do we leave our bodies at night? The astral plane is a good place to solve problems and work out possibilities. In addition, it is the plane we came from and will return to when this life on earth is over. It is home. Sometimes, for example, you meet with another soul to settle a problem on the astral plane that you can't seem to settle on the physical level. You may not remember the meeting at all, or you may have a recollection of some strange or unusually vivid dream sequence involving that person. You may awaken with a feeling that the problem is less important or less demanding then you had thought. It is very likely that the person you have been having difficulties with could call or contact you, starting out with a line like, "I've been thinking," and then offering an idea for a settlement that is mutually acceptable. Or you may suddenly decide this has gone on long enough and you may want to initiate a settlement. When this happens, you can be sure you both met and worked out this settlement while your bodies slept.

Many of my clients have told me of this type of experience. One client has been through a particularly hair-raising divorce with custody problems and financial settlements beyond belief. The legal bills for both her and her ex-husband had been increasing to the point where neither of them would have anything left from the sale of their house, a sizeable sum. She finally decided to contact her ex in the astral plane to try to solve some of the problems and stop the legal merry-go-round.

She pictured his face and said, "Keith, we need to talk tonight." She repeated this three times in a row for three nights. On the fourth morning, she woke feeling everything would finally be OK. She couldn't remember any dream; she just knew something had happened. She called and told me this, and my Spooks told her she would hear that afternoon. Her lawyer called that afternoon, saying a settlement had been offered by her ex-husband through his attorney that morning. It wasn't perfect, but it was much better than any previous agreement. The attorneys would have been happy to continue, but she accepted the proposal and stopped the games.

No one, except my client, could understand why he had suddenly changed his mind. She thanked her Spooks for their help at the eleventh hour. She had really reached the end of her rope, both financially and emotionally, to the point she had been praying that her ex would die in a car accident or worse. She hadn't contemplated suicide because she had custody of their two children, but she was really getting desperate. When she asked for logical help rather than vengeance, the problem was solved.

The funny part is that now she is such a confirmed believer in her own Spooks and abilities she uses the word "Spooks" as her password on everything. I've met her and her children in person and I'm pleased to call them friends. She calls me "Aunt Alice."

## *Plan to Work Out Problems*

When you become aware of your ability to work out problems while sleeping, you can ask your Spooks for help in arranging this before you go to sleep at night. Think of the person you wish to make contact with, visualize his face, and then repeat, "I am going to meet with (insert name)." Do this three times in a row and ask your Spooks to help. Then imagine a good feeling and a good agreement, with both of you smiling—almost like you are watching the whole thing happen on television. You repeat it three times, once for your body, once for your mind, and once for your soul. This programs the brain to allow the contact and sends the need and desire out into the astral plane, much like a prayer.

It may take a couple of nights to actually happen, but it can be arranged. Think of it as a committee made up of your Spooks, the other person's Spooks, and the two of you. It's really a jury of your peers, and our Spooks and guides are so much wiser than we are! They can see the whole picture, not just our own biased side. Try it the next time you are really worried about the outcome of a specific problem.

In some cases you will actually remember the meeting as a very vivid dream. It depends on how clear you are, and how easy it is for you to start using your psychic abilities. We all have this ability; it is part of the other 90 percent of our brains that we don't normally use. It just takes a little practice. This is a form of astral projection you can start using right away.

You can work out a lot more on the astral plane than simply conflicts with other people. Sometimes you have a problem to solve that only you can decide. It might be just a choice or a personal challenge of your own. Examples: Should I buy this car, make that investment, start a new career, go back to school?

You can ask your guides to help you see the alternatives and results from various choices that could be made. But only work on one problem at a time or one in a night! If you mix up the questions, you may not be able to sort out the answers.

Answers come in various ways. You may have a very vivid dream, like watching something on television in which you are the main character, playing the leading role. The result may not be so obvious, but you'll wake up knowing which decision to make. It may even be an alternative that you hadn't thought of yet. Either way you wake up with peace of mind and can't even believe you had thought it was really such a problem. Remember, too, that sometimes deciding not to decide at that moment is the best decision. You may not have all the facts yet.

Years ago I would stay awake half of the night worrying about a particular problem and finally come to some big decision at 2:00 or 3:00 AM. When I awoke at 6:00 AM, I would realize the decision I had made in the middle of the night usually wasn't worth a damn in daylight. I finally understood that the best choice was to send the problem up to my guides and ask for their help. Invariably, I would wake with a truly logical answer to the problem and not have lost most of a night's sleep, tossing, turning, and worrying.

The next time you find yourself in this turmoil, think, "OK, Spooks, I need your help. Let me know what you think in the morning." Then, give them the chance to answer your question. The real YOU will get together with them while your body is asleep and figure it out!

## *True OBEs*

Some individuals are able to astrally project at will. They plan where they want to go, who they will see, and what they will do. If you are able to overcome the fear of what you may experience, you will be able to remember everything in vivid detail. Astral projection is just one step from terminating the connection with your physical body that occurs when we die. This is what people experience when they have an "out-of-body experience." Very simply, when you actually do die, your soul or astral body is out of your physical body and the silver cord is disconnected, so you head for the light and go home. When you sleep or astrally project, the silver cord remains intact and you can't sever it accidentally or on purpose.

One night I decided I would try to do astral projection. Well, I succeeded, kind of, but scared myself very badly and never tried again. I can only describe the sensation I experienced as being tied to the hood ornament on a car and flying very fast just above street level facing the pavement. I could not control my movements or get out of the situation, so I just returned into my body with a bang! I also decided that once was enough. I know this is not typical, and the Spooks needed to let me know this wasn't my thing. I don't teach it or encourage trying to learn how to do this, but I understand it can be done. Just don't ask me to help you!

I do know others are able to astrally project at will and books have been written on this subject, but most people avoid admitting this ability and won't discuss it. There have been too many situations in the past questioning the validity of this ability. Some medical researchers with outstanding credentials have lost their credibility in trying to prove how and why the soul leaves the body. It is the same as trying to prove you have a soul, but individuals who have had an out-of-body experience never forget it and never fear death again. It's like they get a "preview of coming attractions" and like what they see.

## You Practice "Dying" Every Night

Like the country song "I'm coming home, I've done my time . . ." We will all go home someday. The astral plane is our home now. The earth is our center of education, our "School of Hard Knocks." We get to go home from school each night when we sleep. This may be why people who are suffering from sleep deprivation have so many problems. They aren't getting to go home to the astral plane to rest. Incidentally, we are aware of the length of time we agreed to spend on earth during this incarnation, but that is one of the memories we are not allowed to retain in the physical plane. It would prove far too distracting if you knew when you were going to die.

Yet, since we have all experienced the feeling, the comfort and weightlessness just as we fall asleep, we have all practiced astral projection, or the process of dying, many times. Most people who have had an out-of-body experience, which they remember in detail, no longer fear dying. Many feel they have been cheated by being forced to return to this earth to complete their mission or honor the contract made by their soul prior to birth.

I vividly remember my mother-in-law whispering, with big tears in her eyes, that she had been cheated when she regained consciousness after open-heart surgery. She had continued to live after having a heart attack that destroyed nearly half of her heart. After emergency open-heart surgery on Christmas Eve, she regained consciousness five days later, but her mind was stuck somewhere in the past. Her grandson was an uncle, her husband was her father, and I was a babysitter for her own children who were still tiny and at home. She slowly came forward in time until one morning she finally awoke to find herself in the hospital, two months later, with no recollection of what had happened, just a huge scar on her chest.

She really didn't have a vivid memory of an out-of-body experience, but she said with big tears and heartbreak in her voice, "I feel cheated. They told me I had to come back. I didn't want to but I had to." I asked her why they said she had to come back and she replied that she hadn't been a good enough wife. I remember telling her this was ridiculous because she spoiled her husband rotten. (Years later I realized what the guides had meant.) She also couldn't explain who they were, just a "they." She must have spent a long time in the astral plane or on the other side, because she was mentally gone from us for nearly two months. This was many years ago, long before open-heart surgery was an everyday occurrence.

Some of the knowledge gained from her surgery was written up in medical journals and helped the progress made in that field. This must have been part of the reason for her refusing to die until the doctors agreed to try the experimental surgery. They had waited twenty-three days after the heart attack, expecting her to die every day. It must have taken a lot of strength for her soul to agree to be the guinea pig for this surgery and also to come back to this earth afterward. It would be necessary for her to live to have the surgery accepted so others could benefit in the future, but still she must have had a lot of courage. Eight years later, she had to undergo open-heart surgery again to repair new damage.

A similar situation happened to my sister a number of years ago. She had been very sick returning from a trip to Alaska, and doctors later determined that she probably had Rocky Mountain Spotted Fever from a tick bite. They stopped at several cities to get emergency treatment at various hospitals and finally made it home. She had gone to bed with a raging fever and awoke at 3:00 AM from a very vivid dream, drenched in sweat.

In the dream, she was standing on a beautiful mountaintop overlooking miles of terraced gardens that resembled Machu Picchu in Peru. Someone was standing next to her, radiating peace, love, and contentment. The man, dressed in glowing white robes, said, "Juanita, this is your new home." She told him it was beautiful, everything she had ever wanted, but, she asked, "What about 8005 Circle Oaks Drive?" She was instantly sitting up in her own bed, the fever broken, and mentally kicking herself because she had thought of her home on earth.

She has always felt since that time that the option to die and stay on the other side was given to her, and she made the wrong choice. She said she had just meant what would happen to the house; she didn't consciously want to come back. We teased her because she didn't ask about her husband, children, parents, or any of her family, she just asked this angel or God about her house. She admitted that she really would have chosen to return anyway, since her husband was sick and needed her, but after that night she never feared or questioned death again. She looked forward to returning to that beautiful mountaintop, and I'm sure she did. She and I often discussed this strange dream and wondered if this was an out-of-body experience instead of a dream. (These are really the same thing; the difference is in how you remember them.)

Years later, after she died, she came to her oldest son in a dream and said, "It's all a matter of choices—just what choices we make." He said he wanted to ask her a thousand things, but her husband and our parents were with her and they had somewhere important to go. They traveled and played together on this earth, so heaven only knows what they were up to!

Many books have been written detailing the out-of-body experiences people have had when their physical bodies have died or been close to death. The Spooks say the information contained in these accounts is accurate in most cases, and certainly the desire of our souls to return home is very real. Before the end of this century, medical science will have finally accepted the fact that there really is a soul, even if it can't be surgically removed or repaired. When we are finally able to combine medicine, religion, science, psychology, and biology with our own internal faith, then all will benefit and be more complete. Our egos get in the way of allowing us to accept anything greater than ourselves. Keep in mind that the "wonderfulness of myself" does not exist on the astral plane or in heaven, and start trying to let go of some of that ego now.

I have read that some other countries, particularly during the Cold War, were doing research in teaching and using astral projection in order to spy or obtain information on other countries. Since most of this information is still under wraps, we may never know the truth, but more and more people are proving their psychic ability every day. Perhaps one day we won't feel the need to spy on each other. Since everything is open on the other side there really isn't a need to spy or read the minds of others.

## Suicide: Rarely a Good Idea

The fear of dying is part of the veil of forgetfulness that is drawn so we will be able to succeed in this lifetime. If it were not for this we might decide to escape back to the astral plane via suicide when the going gets rough, rather than seeing the problem through to the end and learning in the process. It is seldom right to commit suicide and stop the learning process of our soul. The Spooks say seldom, because there are some rare circumstances in which suicide is permissible. However, if you attempt suicide and fail, it obviously wasn't your time to go. The only way you can succeed in a suicide is if prior approval has been given by your guides or God and then it might not even be a suicide from the Spooks' point of view.

One wild attempt will usually be stopped until you have had time to reconsider, and you usually do. Some people, however, keep trying to kill themselves until they succeed. If a person is that determined to leave, then they have stopped working on their lifetime goals and are concentrating on an escape route. Your higher self and your Spooks, the others in your soul group, decide to let you come home, though you'll usually have consequences to face from a decision like this.

Consider the possibility that twenty individual souls were waiting in line when you were given the option to be born and return to earth. You were born, lived part of your intended lifetime and then you gave up just as your Spooks or guides had received special approval from God to help, one of those miracles you hear about. What you were experiencing seemed so impossible, but right after you committed suicide you could see the obvious other choice and wished another opportunity. What if a new drug had just been perfected to be released to a small group for trial and it would have cured your disease if you had just waited a while longer? What if you were to be one of the miraculous remissions from cancer you read about? What if you had been chosen to make medical or spiritual history and threw away the opportunity? Only you can decide that the choice to leave at that time is the best for all people involved, not just your own personal choice.

My dad said the only reason he couldn't commit suicide during his long terminal illness and battle with cancer was because he had a very real vision of seeing his soul leaving his body just after he had pulled the trigger and hearing someone saying, "Now you'll have to do it all over again." He wasn't about to agree to start all over again! He had a twenty-two pistol, ammunition, and the capability of committing suicide, but chose not to take that option. Consider a life on earth the same as winning a scholarship to the greatest university in the world, and you will ask everyone for help before dropping out. Your Spooks are with you always and all ways.

On many occasions, I've been called upon by individuals I'm reading for to contact a relative on the other side, especially when they committed suicide or on the anniversary of the suicide death. Quite often the Spook will give me the individual's name or nickname and some very special physical traits or behavior. It might be folded arms, a certain smile or laugh, or a special message. It is very comforting to the person I am reading for to know that their loved one is alive and well on the other side.

One woman I spoke with was contemplating suicide herself, until her son reminded her from the other side that his son, her grandson, needed her and that the grandson would choose to live with her when he reached fourteen years of age. She obviously couldn't leave if she was still needed. He will be fourteen in a couple of years so I'm waiting to see when he comes to live with her and why. She will call, I'm sure.

## *Basic Principle: Free Will*

This probably sounds confusing unless you understand something the Spooks bring up often: free will. You choose and plan your own life, and the lessons your soul needs to learn. You even pick your parents. The one option we all have is called free will. This is the right to change your mind if the circumstances have changed since your original commitment or if you are unsure of your own ability to deal with a set of circumstances.

If we have, through free will, destroyed the options to learn that were available to us at birth, the Spooks and guides on the other side will arrange a way for us to leave. This helps to explain some of the strange accidents that happen when there seems to be no logical reason and also helps to explain some cases of sudden infant death. It may not even be anything you have done—obviously, a tiny baby couldn't have done anything yet—but the growing experience and the opportunities your soul needed have been changed. It may even be a free will choice of another soul on the astral plane not to be born yet, and that soul would have been very important to your life.

Every soul in this world has free will—the choice to make our own choice. Any soul who is, or would be, involved with you in working out your karmic experience has the option to change its mind at any time, and this could lead to total chaos if there weren't some guidelines. There is a price to pay when you change your mind, especially when your change affects so many other souls in your world.

One example of the right to change one's mind involved the birth of a client's oldest child. When Jean was starting her family over forty years ago, she lost her first two babies, then gave birth to the third baby who was perfectly beautiful but was born deaf. Her daughter went to special schools, was just as intelligent as she was pretty, and met her husband at Gallaudet University in Washington, D.C. When Jean's daughter married a deaf man and decided to start her family, she also lost the first two babies, then had a perfectly healthy hearing daughter, followed by two equally healthy hearing sons. All of the children learned to sign. The daughter could speak very well and sign simultaneously by the time she was two, and worked as an interpreter for her parents.

The soul who became Jean's daughter had changed her mind twice about being born before she finally agreed to be born on the third attempt with the deaf disability. She was unsure of her ability to handle the handicap she was planning to carry in this lifetime and decided to terminate and reconsider. The guides say the other two handicaps of the miscarried babies were of a more serious nature. This, since it was her choice, put her in the position of having to experience the same sense of loss her mother, Jean, had felt. This could only be completely understood by the exact loss—losing two children. This was hard on all who were involved, but it shows the possible price of a free-will decision and how a choice could also be involved in the Law of Return.

Sometimes, if a choice is a chance to improve the situation, you might also reap the rewards from instigating the change, such as choosing to let go of a dangerous addiction or not to participate in some illegal activity. When you know the easy choice would be the wrong one, you always have the choice to say "No" with pride and with dignity, just as we are teaching the children now, "Just say NO!" If we would only learn to practice what we preach.

## *Avoid Living Suicide*

Free will is also present throughout your lifetime. You may at any time choose to walk away from your lifetime situation because you are afraid of committing suicide but don't feel you can continue in the present circumstances. When you choose to walk away—say, for example, by going out for a loaf of bread and not returning for twenty years—you may have created more karmic debt and problems than you ever had in the first place.

Sometimes we read in the paper about some individual who just walked away, usually with a quick trip to the store in mind. We joke in our family about going out for a loaf of bread, especially when things are difficult.

One example is a man who lived as a near-hermit in a small town in California for over twenty years. He lived alone, avoided the community, and died alone in a newly plowed field from a heart attack. After his death, they discovered he was a man from a large, wealthy New York family. His business and family pressures had become too great; he had just disappeared while everyone searched for years. It wasn't a case of amnesia. Evidence proved that he knew his identity but chose to ignore it. He just walked away from his money, power, responsibilities, family, and all of his karma. I can't believe that his destitute, lonely life could have been better than dealing with his life plan, but he did have the free will, and the choice to leave New York was his.

We are never given more to handle than we are capable of; it's only our own fears that make us doubt our ability. I know his family would have forgiven him any time he chose to return because I read for his daughter.

## Your Free Will Protects You

Keep in mind, no one can find out anything about you that you don't want known. You are protected by your own free will. No psychic, no matter how good, can actually read your mind. If you choose not to let some things about your past be revealed, those special things will remain a secret. Just don't get conned into revealing something you really didn't want to say.

Some years ago my husband and I were on a talk radio show that allowed people to call in and ask questions. It was fun and they wanted us to return, but I decided it wouldn't be wise. My boss had heard the show and was so afraid that I would read his mind that he avoided me for about two months. He also told me, "It was embarrassing," and he didn't want the community to find out his bookkeeper was some kind of a nut. I never did find out what he had in his past or present that he was so afraid of revealing.

I always give a new client the information about free will and "mind-reading" when I start a reading, along with the confidentiality guarantee.

The names of clients revealed in this book have been changed to protect the innocent or guilty, whichever the case may be, and any family stories are only told with the permission of the individual soul involved.

## You Planned Your Life; Keep At It!

Remember, you planned this whole lifetime. Most people who feel they want to leave do so out of fear or loneliness, but you are never really alone. You brought guides and Spooks with you to help you through the difficult times. Try to remember the last time you really were down or afraid, then remember what happened to turn the whole situation around. It usually comes out fine if you allow a little time to pass and some of the things you thought were so tragic at the time become the things you laugh about years later. These frightening things become the fun stories your family will share and laugh about in the future.

One I particularly remember was the story about "How Mom shot Mark," referring to me and my youngest son, Mark.

We lived in the mountains in San Diego County and our dog had brought a nearly dead opossum into the yard. I decided the only decent thing to do was to shoot the poor thing so it wouldn't suffer anymore. I put my three children (ages two, three, and four) and the dog in the house and instilled in them the fear of coming outside while I was shooting the opossum by telling them I might shoot them by mistake, or the bullet might ricochet.

With everyone safe inside I shot the opossum once and was just pulling the trigger for a second "make sure" shot when the door flew open, and all three children and the dog tumbled down the rock stairs at once. They all immediately scrambled back up the stairs screaming, "Mom shot Mark. She said she would. She shot him."

I ran to the house and found the two-year-old bleeding from a wound in his head and the other two running in circles screaming how I shot him. My first fear was that the bullet had actually ricocheted and hit him. When I investigated the wound it was obviously from a rock at the bottom of the stairs. I bundled up all three children, got in the car and drove thirty miles to town with a cold, wet washcloth on Mark's head. Periodically, I tried to assure the other two I had not shot their little brother. He had fallen on a rock.

You could almost guarantee what would happen when we reached the doctor's office. The children actually fought to get out of the car first so they could run in and tell everyone their mother had just shot their little brother! Both were shouting for everyone in the clinic to hear, "Mom shot him. She said she would and she did!" They repeated this to every nurse, doctor, or patient in the whole building! Thank God that was forty-eight years ago and they didn't call the police first and do a physical examination later.

Mark needed thirteen stitches on that one.

The point is this could have been very traumatic for all of the kids. It was certainly frightening for all of us. The kids could have been scarred for life by this experience or needed therapy later in life. I could have been arrested or investigated by present standards and for several days we worried about the lump on Mark's head. What appeared to be a tragedy at first actually became a funny family story.

Sometimes it is darkest before the dawn, just like the old saying. Trust yourself and your guides. It is always best to remember you are only living in a few moments in time right now. Often, just a good night's sleep makes things easier—especially if you ask your Spooks to help you while you sleep, because they can!

You planned this whole life and the individuals who would share it with you before you were ever born. At that time you could see the big picture and knew you would learn most by living the life you currently share with your group. Stay with the game plan and try to see what you are learning in every situation. Sometimes it's funny, sometimes sad and serious, but your soul is learning and growing every minute of every day. Hang in there, the best is yet to come!

---

**PSYCHIC TIP: SOLVE PROBLEMS WHILE YOU SLEEP**

Try asking your Spooks to help you decide something while you sleep. If you have a serious decision to make, ask them to help you decide in a dream or let you know by morning. You'll be surprised how often it works perfectly.

Write down your question, and the answer your Spooks gave you, then check to see what happened. This will help you to trust them, and your guides will know you are serious.

You can arrange to meet with a particular person to work out a problem by saying, "I am going to meet with (insert name) tonight." Repeat this three times.

If you actually have an OBE, share the knowledge with others. You'll be surprised how many people have had this experience but won't admit it to just anyone. They treat it like seeing a UFO and worry that others will think they're nuts. Don't, however, try to create an OBE. They are always spontaneous and are not just to play with!

## CHAPTER SIX

# Attitudes, Affirmations, and a Little Help from Your Friends

Everyone has heard the saying: "You are what you eat." The Spooks say it would be much more accurate to state "You are what you think." Your attitude affects all phases of your life, including your health and mental capabilities. If you seriously try to change your attitude about a situation, you can change your entire life.

One of the most important tools we have found in teaching other souls is the use of affirmations. Affirmations reprogram what your brain thinks and acts on.

Imagine your brain as a very special, complex computer that accumulates all information exactly as it is input and responds accordingly. Each time you say or think a specific thing, the brain acknowledges and stores the information. We convince ourselves we are in love, depressed, happy, sick, or any other emotional or physical state by repeating the idea or phrase until our brains accept and act on the input.

Anything you think or say and preface with the two words "I am" becomes a direct command to your computer brain. Think how often you tell yourself "I am so depressed"—or dumb, fat, or whatever—in one day, particularly when you are unhappy.

## *How to Change Your Life*

The key to changing your attitude lies in forcing yourself to be aware of what you think or say after invoking the key words "I am." "I am" is the same as the Eastern religions' "Om," the sound that's used in meditations, chants, and prayers. It is the first reference in the Bible to God's name at Exodus 3:14. When Moses asked God's name, the voice from the burning bush replied, "I am that I am."

If you treat these two words with respect and learn to use them as intended, you can accomplish anything! This is the secret to affirmations that really work. Repeat the "I am," followed by a positive word or thought. The one I use every day is "I am healthy, I am happy, I am energized." I am now nearly seventy-one years old—and don't look, act, or feel like it. And, yes, I am healthy, happy, and full of energy.

The important thing to remember when using affirmations is to repeat each phrase three times: once for your body, once for your brain, and once for your soul. My body and mental attitude respond to that command within ten minutes after it is given. This system may seem too simple, but my Spooks say most people try to make things more complicated than necessary. Just believe in your affirmations and they will work for you. They don't have to be long, complicated prayers or demands, just simple words or phrases spoken with a positive attitude.

## *Break the Chain of Negative Thought*

While doing a reading for another psychic one day, she kept repeating the phrase, "But I am so depressed. I can hardly get out of bed. I can't do readings, take care of my family . . ." She continued the list of her physical complaints and kept repeating the "I am depressed" routine. Finally, my Spooks couldn't stand it any longer. I interrupted her continuing list of complaints by telling her that she had totally programmed her brain into depression by using the same phrase at least forty-five times in the past fifteen minutes!

She knew better. She believed and taught the same concepts I do, but she had become so involved in a current problem that she had completely forgotten everything she had learned! (Boy, do I know how easy it is to do this, over and over again.) We discussed the means of clearing out the depression program that she had been impressing on her brain. Trying to get her to break the chain of negative thought was difficult. We spent two hours on the phone. It took a great deal of mind control to force herself to replace the word "depressed" with "happy and healthy" every time the thought started to enter her mind.

The negative, depressed thoughts became stronger each time they were repeated and it took a great deal of serious concentration to overcome them. She succeeded and called two days later, her normal self, and very happy to be out of the swamp of self-pity that she had allowed herself to fall into. She had forgotten that when you are up to your ass in alligators, sometimes you forget your original intention was to drain the swamp. It was a very serious lesson in affirmations for her and a strong reminder and reflection for me. It is so easy to forget to use the valuable tool of positive affirmations that is available to all of us. I find myself doing exactly the same dumb thing. We all do it, even when we know better.

"Practice what you preach" is great advice, and it's something my Spooks remind me of daily.

## Affirmations in Action

The immediate response and use of affirmations has been very successful for a twenty-four-year-old young lady I'll call Judy. When I first talked to Judy, she was working as a governess for the family of a college professor. She really wanted to return to college but wasn't financially able to do so. Her parents refused to continue to help her obtain a college education. Previously, she had wasted her time and their money, failing most of her classes and having fun. She was overweight, unhappy, and had trouble finding male companions. She admitted that she probably shouldn't keep calling and "bugging" men she met, but they never called her and that seemed the only way to get dates, even if it amounted to only a sexual encounter.

We discussed affirmations and using them on her weight problem. I encouraged her to return to school, even if she took only a couple of night classes. I also encouraged her to quit chasing and "bugging" the men in her life. The Spooks said, "Don't call them, don't ask them out. Give the guys a chance to take the initiative." Six months later, she called to say the affirmations were working on her weight. She had also started night classes, but was only getting average grades. Judy had met a couple of men who were just friends. She wondered if she should take the initiative and try to get one of the friends to be more than just a friend.

Once again, we discussed the use of affirmations, this time regarding her grades and the need to concentrate in that area for the present. The message she was to give herself: "I am intelligent, I am able to remember everything I read and hear about X." (Whatever the subject or class name.)

On the subject of her male friends, the Spooks said she needed to learn that men were souls inhabiting a male body. She needed to learn more about men by being just friends at this point. She also needed to learn that you can't make someone love you. If she learned more about the opposite sex and more about herself, then love would come.

The last time I talked to Judy, she had her weight problem under control, had returned to college full time with help from her employer, continued to work part time as a governess, and was pulling straight As. Boyfriends? Three at the moment—and she never chases or calls any man she meets! She has set definite long-term goals for her education and career and just knows the right man will walk into her life when it's time to marry—but not for at least three years. In the meantime, Judy has learned to use affirmations in the positive mode to help her obtain the goals and direction she needs to take.

Judy says the greatest thing she has learned in the past three years was to control her attitudes and thinking with affirmations. The result of "I am slim, trim, and beautiful," was the loss of weight and a better self-image she projected to those around her.

Judy knows and believes she is able to do anything she sets her mind to, and she has now proven this to herself. She is really in control of her future and will never drop out again.

## *Rid Your Life of Butts and Beers*

I have recommended the use of the "I am" affirmations to clients repeatedly over the past years, especially when it involves trying to control the use of cigarettes or alcohol. If you say, "I won't smoke or drink again," it won't work. Your brain does not hear the negatives as "won't, don't, can't," etc. It only hears "I smoke or drink again," immediately acts on that, and helps create a stronger addiction.

I have found that the best system is to say "I am free of cigarettes," or "I am free of alcohol." The word "free" means you are releasing this item (or even a person) back to the universe. You don't crave, need, love, hate, or fear that item or person anymore. Just free the object, addiction, or the person. Say your line three times in a row and it will usually take hold within one week.

This method really helped me to finally break my addiction to cigarettes—and I tried everything for years. I tried the patches that are so popular, but I was so allergic to nicotine that they burned my skin badly. I couldn't continue to use them. Can you even imagine the stubbornness of a soul who insists on using a product that she is so allergic to? I can and did for thirty-four years!

One of my clients was an alcoholic and had been for years. She was experiencing serious liver problems due to the abuse. Even the physical problem and the threat of death hadn't been able to stop her. She started the "I am free" technique and was able to break the lifetime of abuse. It wasn't easy, and she called me for reinforcement many times, even in the middle of the night, but she is finally really free of that addiction. During the process, she fell off the wagon a few times, but climbed right back up, started again, and now appears to be over that problem in this lifetime.

If you want to get rid of an addiction or just a bad habit, try the "I am free" therapy. It doesn't cost a penny and no one knows you are using it. This is just between you and your guides. They will help you.

## *The Power of Beliefs*

My next-door neighbor, Carol, is nearly eighty-two years old. She jogs, rides her bicycle, works in her garden, and works part time at the local hospital as activities director for elderly long-term patients. Some of the patients are younger than she is, but nobody would even guess her age. She also volunteers at the hospital as a hairdresser, giving haircuts and permanents to the patients. As if this isn't enough, she maintains a volunteer program that shampoos and sets hair for all of the female patients once a week. In her spare time, she babysits, cleans houses, and does sewing and craft projects as gifts and as contributions to the various fund-raising activities in the community.

Carol is a very pretty, blond, blue-eyed lady who came to this country from Norway as a seven-year-old child. She is a cosmetologist and owned her own beauty shop for years before retiring to "go to work"! She has lived her life believing that what you think, you become, and she has a great faith in God. The proof of the energizing force behind these beliefs is the vitality and youthfulness she still possesses.

She is a wonderful reflection of what I may be able to become in the next few years. I hope I am strong enough to succeed. Some people in our community have asked if we are sisters, a question I accept as a great compliment.

The old saying, "You're only as old as you think you are," is really true. If you continue to think positive and youthful thoughts, you can maintain your strength and vitality. Carol is living proof.

About fifteen years ago, I had a "Grandma Day" with my four grandsons, then aged six through eight. Grandma Days are when all four would spend the day and night with me in a horrendous sleepover. We planned and did weird things, like taking nature hikes, building forts out in the woods, making a bow and arrows, terrorizing the local playgrounds and stores, and going sledding in the snow or whatever else came to mind for good, clean fun. Or dirty fun—we ended up painting ourselves with mud from head to toe in mush pots. (Mush pots, just in case you are curious, are holes dug into the ground, filled with water and dirt, then stomped to a nice slimy texture, which is then spread from head to foot.)

On this particular day, the boys had decided on tumbling lessons. We placed mats on the floor for padding. I was trying to explain how to do a headstand by placing your head and hands in a triangle position for the base, when I suddenly realized I was not only telling them, I was showing them! Here was a fifty-six-year-old grandmother, standing on her head in the middle of the living room. Grandmas don't do tumbling—do they? I hadn't tried a headstand or cartwheel in years and discovered, much to everyone's surprise, I still could do it.

We went roller skating a couple of months ago, which I was a little dubious of at first, thinking of all the possible accidents. Then I remembered affirmations. "I am able to skate." I did before—why not now? It was great fun, and once again I proved to myself you can do anything you believe you can do, physically and mentally.

## *You* Can *Teach an Old Dog New Tricks*

Two of the things I promised myself I would not learn this lifetime were the metric system and computers. Too confusing. I'm too old and you can't teach an old dog new tricks. Right?

That is only true if you believe it. I had to learn portions of the metric system in one of my last jobs, which was as a bookkeeper and part-time counterperson at a John Deere dealership. To order and sell parts and materials, I had to learn some of the metric system and conversions. In one of my other jobs I was handed a computer with Lotus and WordPerfect on it and was told to learn it. Within two months I had learned how to run the computer and spreadsheet program, rebuilt the company's books for the past two years, set up an accounting system on the computer, and created a complete financial statement to present to the accountant.

There is no way that would have been possible without using affirmations to remember and use the information I was studying. I even borrowed a bit from Edgar Cayce and slept with the computer books under my bed or pillow. With affirmations and help from my Spooks, I'm no longer afraid of learning anything new.

On the other hand, if you think you are old and no longer capable, that is what you will become. A friend was visiting us about eight years ago when we decided to get into my little Nissan truck for a quick sightseeing trip. Since there were four of us, she had to sit in one of the jump seats in the rear of the King cab. (Smallest King cab on the planet.) She had a great deal of difficulty getting in and almost had to be lifted out. Her answer was that after all, she was over fifty, and not expected to climb around like a young kid. Believing that will make her lose her muscle tone and agility faster than any illness. We talked about aging physically and how attitude hastens the aging process.

The message is simple: Think young, stay young, and keep active, or you'll be old long before your time.

## Poor Thinking: Education Comes at a Cost

At times, when I'm carrying an unconstructive attitude, my Spooks take a very interesting, and often expensive, way to point it out to me. If I don't learn fast, they make sure the price of education is high enough that I will remember.

We live in an area where a large herd of mule deer are protected. Since these are large animals and naturally believe they own the territory, deer bouncing along the highways are responsible for many automobile accidents. Dead deer along the roadway, and skid marks, leave evidence of the previous night's slaughter. I've always felt so sorry for the deer and a little angry with the drivers who drive too fast or do not watch the sides of the road carefully enough. I have very good peripheral and distance vision, and I can usually see deer long before there is any danger of hitting one. Because of this, I didn't really believe people needed to hit or kill deer. I never believed the stories that began, "He jumped right out in front of me." I assumed the teller of the tale was either drunk, lying, or speeding. (Talk about an attitude!) My lack of understanding and attitude apparently needed adjusting, and my Spooks were only too happy to oblige.

It was dark when I left the office and the drive home took me over the top of a large mountain, which is home to part of the deer herd. I spotted deer nearly every night and drove slowly. I was often passed by others who apparently didn't share my concern for the deer or the amount of vehicle damage they are capable of causing. I was slowly crawling up the hill behind a semi truck that had just left the plant where I worked, when the driver blinked his lights to indicate it was safe to pass. As I passed the truck, I was thinking about calling the trucker's office the following morning to compliment him on his courtesy. I blinked my lights as a thank you and pulled back over and started to gain some speed. Luckily, my little truck had just started to accelerate when I saw the top six inches of a deer's hindquarters pass my left headlight. I immediately felt the jolt and noticed one of my headlights was pointing toward the sky. I knew I had hit the deer, but it didn't seem that hard. Then I searched for a place to pull over to assess the damage. The entire front end was damaged. The destroyed bumper had a strip of deer hair hanging from it. After determining my pickup was still drivable, I limped home. The repair cost over $2,500 dollars and took one month to get the necessary parts to complete.

The following morning I called the trucking company, told them how much I appreciated the driver's courtesy in blinking for a safe pass. Then I asked them to find out why he had put me on point to hit the deer? They all had a good laugh over that, and the driver assured me that had not been his intention. He had not seen me hit the deer even though he was right behind me. He did notice the deer standing beside the road shaking its head then scrambling up the embankment. Since I had hit the deer exactly in the center of the vehicle, I was barely jostled and completely unharmed. However, my little truck—only four months old—was very badly damaged, and the deer walked away shaking his head.

My attitude received the greatest amount of damage, because I was forced to recognize that some deer really do jump erratically into the line of traffic. It had not been my wonderful vision and superb driving skills that had prevented an accident. It was the protection from my Spooks. My big fat ego had been raising its ugly head. Another blow to the "wonderfulness of myself."

Since that incident, I continued to drive the same highway for seven more years, but I never forgot who is protecting me and the deer. I also have much more sympathy for those involved in accidents.

## *Heed Warnings Well*

I've read for one client for a very long time. She didn't pay me for the first reading, however, because she didn't like what the Spooks told her. Then she called back about two months later, very angry because what the Spooks had warned her to beware of had happened.

She was dating a man who was a heavy drinker. She also liked to drink, so she chose to continue to see him even though he was very abusive and obviously using her. He encouraged her addiction to alcohol, which was starting to take over her life. The Spooks told her to be very careful because this man had a disease that was transmitted by sex and she could catch it. Their recommendation: Stop the relationship and run like hell! I had never heard anything like that from the Spooks before.

She refused to pay me until she called back to tell me that she had tested positive for Hepatitis C. The man eventually admitted he knew he had it. He just didn't believe he could give it to anyone else, regardless of what modern research had proven. When confronted, he at first told her she was probably cheating on him and had caught it elsewhere. He said the whole thing was just her plot to discredit him and broke off the relationship immediately. Then she found out he was already seeing someone else. She contacted the other woman to warn her about the hep C, but the other woman would not believe her. She thought it was jealousy.

She now has hepatitis C and probably will for the rest of her life. She has given up drinking, however, and has helped herself with the "I am" affirmation therapy. She is working on trying to cure the hep C with affirmations and herbal medications. She is also much more discriminating about who she dates or gets involved with and has continued to stay away from alcohol because of the liver problems. She drank heavily before she got involved with this man, drank with him, and has now been forced to let that addiction go because of the liver damage.

We all learn eventually, with some of us learning the hard way. She calls often, is really a good person, and has been left with the unhappy situation of being required by law to notify anyone she gets involved with that she has hepatitis C and they could become infected. This has really changed her lifestyle.

So if you get a warning from a friend or somebody's Spook to be careful—*be careful.*

## *Ask for Help*

The incident with the deer yielded another lesson. It reminded me of how my Spooks speak to me constantly—if only I take the time to listen.

I can drive the road with my mind on seventeen million other things, but, when I suddenly think "deer" they will be on the highway or next to it within a few hundred feet. Occasionally it is not a warning, but just a wake-up call, so I'll pay attention in time to enjoy a beautiful sight like a large buck deer silhouetted by an orange sunset a mile in front of me.

Another thing the Spooks do is make me suddenly think "snake" just in time to miss stepping on one. I can be out running with my grandsons, playing, doing whatever insane thing we are doing at that moment when the thought comes into my mind. I don't question it; I just warn the kids to watch out. One is nearby, and we usually see it, but since they are not deadly we live and let live.

The first time I ever had that experience, I was ten years old and coming up to the main house from the little cabin I slept in. Suddenly, my mind said "snake," and I was able to lengthen my stride by just enough to miss stepping on a six-foot-long rattlesnake, sunning himself in the pathway. I landed on the run, told my father, and he brought a gun to shoot the rattler. It was real, it was there, and it was large enough with enough venom to have possibly killed me. I never forgot and always looked when my Spooks said "snake" again. Obviously they were talking to me back then. I just did not recognize what was happening.

Besides listening to such wake-up calls, you can and should ask for protection when you think you need it.

A simple request for protection while driving, for example, is enough to receive it. If you don't feel comfortable asking your Spooks for protection, then try imagining a white light around your car or the vehicle of someone you love and want to protect. It's the same thing and maybe easier to do.

Our daughter drove over this same mountain every day to take her children to school. They enjoyed watching the deer, but they never encountered problems in near misses or accidents. However, she had some concerns regarding other vehicles tailgating her. When another vehicle gets too close all she has to do is ask in her mind that it allow more space and the other driver immediately backs off. Debbi is not sure how her Spooks arrange contact with the other driver, but it works every time.

## *Spooks Do Intervene Upon Occasion*

Recently, Debbi's Spooks almost didn't get her attention soon enough. She was gently rear-ended by a fully laden logging truck, one of the big fears of anyone driving these mountain roads. (Nobody is gently rear-ended!) She had been stopped by a Cal Trans Road Construction crew and was the last car in line waiting for the pilot car.

Her Spooks warned her to look behind her quickly. In the rear-view mirror she could see a log truck coming fast. He apparently had not noticed the construction signs, and she suddenly realized he was not going to stop in time. She considered trying to get out of the way to either side but realized there wasn't time and there was no place to go. Since she always allows extra space between her and a car in front, she removed her foot from her brake to allow the car to absorb some of the forward motion that would be generated by the crash, then slammed on the brake right after being hit. This resulted in moving forward enough to allow the truck driver to come to a stop at the same time she did. Her bumper had just been kissed, and the car in front of her wasn't even touched.

The truck driver was aware of what had happened. He had watched helplessly while Debbi brought the situation under control. His face was as white as this paper. He knew how close they had all come to becoming another highway statistic. Debbi knows her reactions are good, but not that good. The Spooks took control of the vehicles for those few seconds or Debbi would have been sandwiched between the log truck and the chain of traffic. Even the highway patrolman told her she had someone looking out for her. Yes—her Spooks. Debbi thanks them and appreciates them every day.

They rode with her every time she drove on a 240-mile round trip to Klamath Falls, Oregon, while she was enrolled in a nursing program. She felt their protection, almost like a force field surrounding her car. There was, she said, a pillar of light off to each side in the rear and one directly in front of the car, like a triangle. She watched a deer run up to the field in front of her car and actually be deflected off to the side of the road unharmed.

Rockie and I once returned from a trip where the Spooks did the driving, guiding the car through about six inches of mud and snow, pulling us out of skids and delivering us safely in both directions. It's an unbelievable sensation to feel the car start to skid and then feel a steadying hand take over the steering. We don't drive fast as the Spooks don't let us, but we nearly always see other cars off to the side of the road or headfirst into a snow bank, which leaves no doubt as to the condition of the road.

Another morning the Spooks prevented a terrible accident by controlling my daughter-in-law's car when we hit black ice while driving her children to school. It was a long stretch of icy highway, since we had a conversation while sliding. I was trying to hold both grandsons while checking the fields alongside the road for the least dangerous crash site to head for. When I tried to explain that to Kathy, she said, "To heck with the kids. Help me control this darn car!" I reached over and put one hand on the steering wheel and the skid immediately stopped. I knew it wasn't my touch. It was our guides who intervened at that moment and saved us from injury.

I believe you can obtain help from your Spooks just by acknowledging their presence and asking for their help. If it is possible to intervene and prevent an accident or injury, I'm sure they will in most cases. The only reason they might not be able to help would be if the resulting injury or legal ramifications are part of a bigger karmic plan that would involve you working through a series of events due to a karmic debt or maybe even a positive event.

Remember, events like accidents are always planned by you and if the bigger picture requires a specific problem that would be put in motion by the accident, your Spooks can't prevent it. Doing so would alter events and change the life plan, your life plan.

---

**PSYCHIC TIP: HOW TO HEAR YOUR SPOOKS**

You can hear your Spooks speaking to you through your nighttime dreams, daydreams, unexpected thoughts that invade your conscious train of thoughts, or even a voice. It is not your imagination. If listening requires you to change your direction, do it.

Tip: Write down your dreams. Messages often come in them.

Tip: If a thought comes into your mind, out of the blue, try to figure out why. Look around you and pay attention!

The Spooks say we ignore them too often. We try to give credit to our imagination or just our wishes. Did it ever occur to you that your imagination might be fed in part by your guides?

# CHAPTER SEVEN

# Healing with Color and Alternative Medicine

In every account of an out-of-body experience or psychic event, something is mentioned about the radiant and beautiful colors on the astral and other planes. Apparently, the colors we see on earth are a poor imitation of the real colors created by God. My own experience in working with colors, for healing or for readings, is that astral colors are more vivid, almost neon in intensity, with a depth and clarity that can't be described. We just don't have the words.

## *Healing Energies*

Some years ago, I broke my foot at work. It was poor timing. I was changing to a new job in two days and just couldn't show up with a broken foot. A bone surgeon verified the break, a small bone on the bottom of my foot, with an x-ray. He suggested I stay off it for a week and soak it. He told me that if it started hurting or swelling too much, he would have to put a cast on it. No way! I started working on affirmations to heal my foot, like "I am healing my foot." I asked all of my Spooks, God, and everyone else I knew on the other side to help.

It wasn't working.

My youngest son Mark had heard about my broken foot in town and dropped by to check. He offered to help me heal it and I grabbed the offer. While he held the foot in both of his hands, I continued to concentrate on healing affirmations, when suddenly I saw a blinding flash of red light—with my eyes closed. I kept them closed. I didn't want to lose this beautiful color. It started doing figure eights into and through my foot. There was an arrow on one end and long, beautiful streamers on the other. It changed colors from red to violet to purple, then to brilliant blue, aqua, and green. It remained green for some time, then gradually blended into yellow, faded to white, and disappeared.

My foot quit hurting completely. I opened my eyes and sat there grinning as my son continued to concentrate while holding my foot. Suddenly, my toes started doing some strange dance of their own, totally out of control. I laughed out loud and told my son it was healed. He replied, "Yes, I know. I'm just clearing out the last bit of congestion." I got up and walked around the room, totally cured. I knew my son was a healer, could see auras, and was very psychic. But I had never been the recipient of this form of psychic healing before. It was unbelievable.

## *Healing Is Self-Healing*

I believe the purpose of the injury I just described was to teach me the process of healing by colors, so I could pass it on to other people. This process heals. It is limited only by your own faith and belief. It can stop pain and help to cure many things. One girl I read for tried it and was able to prevent surgery on her thyroid and totally clear the problem. Another healed her knee after a skiing accident and avoided surgery. Many others have been cured of a multitude of illnesses and physical problems.

And I didn't heal them—they healed themselves using this method. I did not even stay on the phone with them while they used the system. They did it alone. No matter what method is used, healing is always self-healing. It doesn't matter who the person is who is working on you, if you don't have faith in the method or person, you won't be healed. (Nor will you be healed if you don't want to be healed, but more on that in a few pages.) You have to allow the process to work, believe it will, and it will. The Bible is filled with various stories of healing and Jesus is supposed to have said, "By your own faith, you have been healed."

And I've used the process myself. Earlier, I described how I had a cancerous melanoma on my back. When it was removed, I felt absolutely no pain and the cancer has never recurred. I used the color sequence to stop the cancer myself. Maybe I did stop the spread of the disease, because the doctor said it was completely encapsulated when he removed it. You must remember, I didn't think or believe it would be cancerous and kidded the doctor about it being a melanoma so I probably wasn't really taking it as seriously as I should have before the diagnosis.

When it was diagnosed as a melanoma, I got very serious and worked on it repeatedly while I went through the process of seeing a skin specialist (who recommended that I come back every six months to be looked at). I refused both radiation and chemotherapy. I didn't want to have either of those treatments and felt if it was my time to go, I was ready. I was willing to accept what the Spooks sent me, but I still used the healing colors intermittently for several years. If I didn't get to go home, I at least didn't want to be disabled, but I would have left quite happily.

## *The Sequence of Colors Matters*

If you have a malady of any kind, try it yourself. Imagine the beauty and the healing colors I described.

The sequence of the colors is significant because it shows the direction of thought in the healing process. Red indicates the physical life situation and acknowledges the pain and injury to the body. Violet and purple indicate the pity and hurt, which turns into blue, meaning truth and reality. As you change from blue to shades of green you are in the actual healing field. As this changes to yellow you have acknowledged, intellectually, the healing process has taken place, and the color becomes white, showing purity of mind. Then it changes to clear to indicate the problem has passed. ("Clear" is like a window pane. Something is there, but you can see through it. A clear color is a space that is defined by sparkling and twinkling dots to show there is a boundary and something inside, even if it appears to be a blank area.)

Other colors may also be used in different forms of healing, but these are the only ones I was given that night.

As you look at the following color chart, you can follow the sequence of colors I described as the Spooks gave them to me. While the healing was actually taking place, I wasn't thinking of the color, meanings, or sequence—just how incredibly beautiful they were. These had to be the colors from the astral plane.

## Colors, Attitudes, and Auras

| | | |
|---|---|---|
| Clear | * | Seeing clearly; good perception |
| White | * | Purity of mind; good disposition |
| Silver | ** | Spiritual goodness |
| Glitter | ** | Glamour; showy; outstanding |
| Yellow | * | Intellectual; clear and open-minded; spiritually inclined |
| Yellow-Brown | | Cowardice; weak |
| Orange | | Pride; ambition; go getter |
| Dark Orange | | Too aggressive |
| Pink | ** | Love; empathy; tenderness |
| Red | * | Zest for life; enjoys life; physical plane |
| Bright Red | | Too sensual |
| Scarlet | | Scornful; hateful; conniver |
| Lavender | * | Sympathetic; pity |
| Purple-Gray | | Self-pity |
| Purple-Blue | * | Spiritual thoughts |
| Blue | * | Truth and reality; noble; honorable |
| Dark Blue | ** | High religious feelings |
| Emerald Green | ** | Versatility; ingenuity; creativity |
| Pale Green | * | Sympathy; compassion; healing |
| Green-Brown | | Jealousy; envy |
| Brown | | Antagonistic; picky |
| Dark Brown | | Miserly; selfish |
| Gray | | Depression; fear |

Black                    Hatred or malice; curiosity if shiny or reflective (black with streaks of red indicates anger)

Colors can have other meanings. This chart shows attitudes and colors that appear in the aura and that are used in the healing process. I have placed an asterisk by those used in this type of healing. Those with the double asterisk are used in other psychic healing processes.

## *The Symbolic Side of Injuries or Illness*

Pain or discomfort in an area of your body may be associated with an attitude or a challenge in your life. You're often not aware, for example, that a runny nose and sinus problem could be related to a problem you are having trouble facing. The chest cold and congestion might be eliminated if you are able to "get something off your chest."

The following is a list of possible medical problems and the feelings or thoughts that could be aggravating the situation. This list also includes "accidents," something the Spooks say are very rare.

| Physical Manifestation | Attitude or Feeling |
| --- | --- |
| Smashed thumb | Will; doing something against your will |
| Index finger injured | Pointer; making a point |
| Middle finger | Anger; sexual frustration |
| Ring finger | Relationships; marriage problems |
| Little finger ("pinky") | The "little" things in life |
| Right hand | Giving; male attitude or side of a personality |
| Left hand | Receiving; female side of a personality |
| Feet | Balance or out of balance |
| Legs | Direction |
| Knees | Being brought to your knees |
| Back | Burdens to carry |
| Shoulder | Work; putting your shoulder to the wheel |

Throat sore or hoarse   Wanting to say something

Chest cough      Getting something off your chest

Most of these meanings are pretty obvious. We often have sayings that reflect our intuitive knowledge about the cause of illnesses or physical ailments: "I just can't stomach the mess," or, "My boss is a pain in the neck."

The next time you smash your thumb while doing a project that you really didn't want to do at that moment, it will make you laugh when you realize why it happened. Small children quite often have heavy wax build-up in their ears, especially if they are being told no a lot or if they don't want to hear what they are being told. We all do things subconsciously to our bodies. Some things are very minor, while other things can be much more serious. Positive attitudes, affirmations, and some help in healing can do a lot to improve our health.

## *Alternative Healing Methods*

There are many types of psychic healing being used today. Some involve methods used for centuries in India, Tibet, Japan, and other areas of the world. The ones I've heard most about recently are the Reiki and crystal techniques. There are many books on both subjects available today. So many alternative forms of medicine are beginning to be accepted. It seems that we will all profit from this new acceptance of old knowledge—healing methods that had been used several generations ago. Acupuncture and acupressure are both gaining in use and acceptance in the Western world now.

When my daughter's husband was so sick with cancer, she placed a large crystal on the headboard of the bed, pointed directly at the place where he slept. The interior of the crystal shattered into tiny fractures throughout. The exterior still looked intact, but the inside was fragmented. This was very indicative of what was happening inside his body due to the cancer. We still have the crystal but it is now retired.

## *Alternative Medicine: The Deeper Story*

Alternative medicine is a misnomer. It is as old as the history of this planet. If anything, Western medicine should be called alternative medicine. However, for the sake of clarity, I will refer to anything other than Western medicine as alternative medicine.

Most alternative healthcare means and methods are very much like the old home remedies grandma used. They comprise herbs, medicinals, compresses, plasters, etc., that have been passed down through generations. The Aborigines in Australia are the oldest surviving tribe in earth history. They did not rely on Western medicine in any form. Obviously, they were quite successful in their treatments. American Indians, South American indigenous tribes, and African tribes have many forms of alternative healthcare and medicines. They were around for many years prior to our Western medicine.

The same is true of all heritage lines. Examples include using an egg white to draw an infection in the skin to a head (pustule), eucalyptus oil for congestion, foxglove for irregular heart rate (digitalis comes from foxglove), or hawthorn for high blood pressure or low blood pressure. There are so many that there are volumes of books on medicinals, herbals, aromatherapy, body manipulation, massage, and the list goes on.

Most of our wonderful medicine chest at home comes from variations of herbs, trees, and plants taken from the jungles in the world or old folklore remedies passed down and spruced up through generations. Examples are aspirin, Milk of Magnesia, Bag Balm, and Witch Hazel, to name just a few.

Yet modern drugs and medications can be really fantastic, unless you happen to be allergic to them. Years ago, Rockie came down with pneumonia that started with valley fever. They were not able to diagnose the source of the pneumonia until the second trip to the hospital. By that time, Rockie was in critical condition, because he was allergic to all of the various types of antibiotics they tried on him. The treatments on his re-admission were old-fashioned mustard packs, aspirin, and an oxygen tent. They didn't know what to do, but he made it through the night and by the following day they found a new antibiotic he was able to tolerate.

A combination of the old "alternative" treatment and a new antibiotic saved him. He later lost two lobes of his right lung due to the extent of the valley fever infection and damage. If we had known more about healing treatments at that time, it would have been much easier and maybe saved him a lot of pain.

Now there are literally hundreds of different alternative treatment modalities available. They even teach hands-on healing in the nursing schools now. Ten or twenty years ago, this was not even discussed, much less practiced.

## Alternative Healing: A Success Story

One type of diagnosis and treatment was completed on my son-in-law (the one treated in part by the crystal described above). It actually brought him back from death's door with cancer. He had been reduced to skin and bones, lost sixty pounds, and was dying when a physician who also believes and practices alternative medicine started the treatment.

He had prostrate cancer and a multitude of serious lung problems. The physician who treated him successfully used homeopathic medicinals and vitamins, but administered them by IV daily over a period of six weeks. It was very intensive, but it worked. We know three other people personally who experienced the same success from that physician using those treatments. My son-in-law has regained his weight and strength in the five years since the treatment and leads a normal life now at the age of seventy-eight.

He just installed new brakes on his car yesterday—by himself.

## The Right Treatment: Whatever Works for You

Many progressive medical centers now offer both forms of treatment, Western and Eastern or alternative medicine. Which is better? Whichever one works for you.

When I get too involved in natural healing and affirmations, my Spooks often get me to acknowledge Western medicine by causing some totally unexplainable illness. Just recently, I went to the clinic where my daughter works as a nurse practitioner on weekends. I woke in the morning with my face and eyes swollen and increasing difficulty breathing. It was apparently an allergic reaction to some unknown substance. Two shots and a breathing treatment later I was released with the reaction under control.

I don't know what the source of the allergic reaction was, but I'm willing to bet the Spooks wanted me to recognize and appreciate the need for Western medications. I do, and strongly recommend you also use these treatments when necessary.

Alternative medicine is less invasive and usually allows the body to heal itself with treatments, herbs, and visualization therapy. On occasion, people have been able to avoid surgical procedures by use of alternative medicine techniques. In the past, women usually gave birth with the assistance of a midwife or family member rather than a doctor in the hospital. We still have midwives practicing today and many of them work with doctors in hospitals. They have successfully combined both types of medicine.

When we are able to combine the various forms of medicine and healing, we all benefit. Many of the prejudices and jealousies that existed in the past between the different fields of treatment have been clearing in recent years. This had also been predicted to occur after the turn of the century. Maybe this is the good part of the Y2K changes.

## First: Look for the Cause of the Illness

Over the years, the Spooks and I have done readings for many individuals who have become excellent healers working in many of the healing modalities now used.

One individual called me many years ago. She was working in one of the big department stores, was having trouble with chest pain and difficulty in breathing. And she hated her job—to the point that she was very clearly telling her body that she would rather die than continue working in it. The Spooks stated clearly that the stress and pressure would lead to a heart attack if she didn't do something to change her life or her job.

Imagine my surprise when she called me back the next day, saying she had just given notice and would be leaving that job within ten days. The Spooks said she was a natural healer and needed to work with other people. She already knew massage therapy, but took a class in and was certified in reflexology in her state. She started working part time in a center that worked with many forms of healing. She loved the work, was happy, and healthy.

The other bonus she obtained, quite unexpectedly, was that when she quit, she withdrew all of her stock and options with the big department store. She was forced to cash in all of the retirement package and ended up with a very nice reserve and nest egg. It was not enough to retire on completely, because she was still too young, but it was certainly a safety net for the future. The Spooks hadn't even mentioned this benefit, but the reserve had always been there and she just hadn't realized how much it came to.

The unusual thing was that the stock market ended up dropping considerably during the next few months and the amount she was able to cash in would have been reduced about 70 percent if she had continued to work for that employer. This was an extra bonus; she has always given the Spooks credit for pushing her into doing something at that moment.

She continued to work in the healing center and increase her clientele until she was working just about full-time. Suddenly, some outside influences caused the healing center to close and once more she was unsure of what her future might be. The Spooks said she was a healer and needed to remain in that field and suggested she go into business for herself. I kept hearing the words from the movie "Field of Drems" running through my head, and told her, "If you build it, they will come." She finally realized that she could remodel her basement and turn it into a healing and therapy room with very little expense. Besides, she had the nest egg from the department store job if needed.

She was still quite fearful, however, because her home was twenty miles out of town. The Spooks told her it didn't matter. People would be willing to travel the distance to be able to see her and kept repeating, "If you build it, they will come." She did, and they did. She's had all the clients she can handle and no one has ever complained about the distance. Some individuals even like the confidentiality they maintain because there are no homes close to hers, so no one can see who comes and goes.

She has become so well known and worked on so many different cases that people even come from other states to see her.

When I first started reading for her, she helped me to get a swift kick from my Spooks and to realize it wasn't always my thoughts or my voice during a reading. During the reading, she had made a statement that I considered very unreasonable and I heard myself saying, "That makes about as much sense as talking to the spider in the corner!"

There was absolute silence, and then she whispered, "How did you know I talked to the spider in the corner?" It was my turn to be surprised, because I didn't know why I had said that. It was certainly not something I'd ever even thought of in the past. It proved the Spooks were able to deliver a remark that meant something to the person I was reading for to prove a point. It also proved to me that the Spooks really were in charge. They love to do that!

It turned out that she had a huge spider in the corner by the door on the front porch and she talked to the spider quite often. Since then I've come to realize that she also talks to ants, bugs, various animals and nature's creatures all of the time. I sometimes wonder if she is a bit of a leprechaun. She is very in tune with Mother Nature and even knows when an earthquake will occur and how bad it will be. Not where, but she'll have an unusual feeling for several days in advance. Not enough to help predict them with any guarantees, just a strange, nauseated, dizzy, or disoriented feeling.

She has also proven that distance is no object when it comes to using her healing abilities. My son had been in severe pain for over a week with a kidney stone. He had seen the doctor repeatedly and was on pain medication. I called and asked what portion of the foot represented the kidney area and if there was anything she could suggest that might help him. She immediately described the portion of the foot and then said we needed to find a small round ball or, better yet, a knobby doggy chew toy. She then proceeded to describe the new chew toy my daughter's little dachshund puppy had, even the color. She told me to have my son roll the toy around the sole of his foot with enough pressure to feel the small knobby protrusions. At that point, he would have stood on his head and chewed the toy himself if it would have given him some relief. He did as she suggested, and the next morning the kidney stone passed out of his system. He was able to take it to the lab for examination, so it wasn't his imagination.

Recently, I asked if she knew of anything to ease the pain of my rheumatoid arthritis in my wrists and thumbs. She said she had created an herbal concoction that relieved pain and sent me a sample. When I called to let her know it had really helped, I asked what was in the product. She laughed and said she had just flown her broom over the cauldron an extra time or two. I couldn't care less. It eases the pain, smells great, and I've ordered several refills. (She really doesn't practice witchcraft. It's just an inside joke.)

Apparently, the symptoms she had when she first called (shortness of breath, chest pain) disappeared right after she left the department store. She has had no further symptoms or physical problems. The purpose of the whole thing was to get her working as the excellent healer she is. She refers clients to me all the time for a reading, so I often hear about some of her nearly miraculous healings from them. She never tells me about her healing treatments (her clients do) and I never discuss their personal readings with her. We maintain the confidentiality we promise to our clients, and the clients know we will!

Why can't I heal my own arthritis using the color method? I've tried, but it has not worked so far, but it may be that I have never spent much time or concentrated on it enough to completely cure the problem. Rheumatoid arthritis is chronic and genetic in my family and so far I've had little success in healing genetic disorders. Maybe we choose or agree to carry these ailments for a portion of our lives, just like the migraine headaches. Maybe the illness teaches something about compassion and respect for physical problems. The Spooks say repeatedly,

"What you don't understand, you have to wear," and I have memories of being pretty certain some of these medical problems were "all in their heads" on several occasions.

If karma is involved, you won't be relieved of the problem until the lesson is learned. Remember your free will is involved, and some things you have to personally experience to really understand. It's just that we usually pick the hard way! Besides, maybe I was supposed to be a patient for the herbal treatment the healer sent to me.

## *Your Health, Your Choice*

One of the most important things to remember and work on when using healing techniques is the intertwining of the psychological and physical aspects of your body and mind. You really are what you think! This is the difficult part of healing yourself. You have to be honest with yourself about what is really bothering you and what you believe will cure the problem. You also have to be honest with yourself if you don't really want to be cured.

One woman for whom I've read for a long time had an injury caused by her work. The problem involved her shoulder and had been accelerating for four years. She didn't want to return to the type of work she was doing, ever, and though not being consciously aware of it at the time, she made sure she would never have to. The problem with her shoulder had been intensified to the point that it required surgery and rehabilitation. The rehab was to retrain her in another field so she would not need to go back to the original job. She now realizes what part her attitude played in the final outcome, but this is what she was supposed to do. (Even not being aware of it at the time it was happening was part of the package!)

She is a healer and is able to offer a lot of relief to others, but she couldn't stop the process of surgery and therapy for herself. I worked with her repeatedly, using the "I am" healing techniques, but nothing seemed to help or stop the damage from the injury. We were able to gain some relief from pain for her, but not able to stop the process.

She has been retrained in the healing techniques, such as visualization, Reiki, and herbal medications. She is not physically able to do massage therapy since it requires more strength than she has in that shoulder, but that's fine because she prefers the other forms of alternative healing. Her desire to change her entire lifestyle, even though the intent was buried deep inside her subconscious mind, was enough to prevent psychic healing. This required her to go through the various surgeries to regain partial use of that shoulder.

In the long run, she really got what she wanted and needed in this life time, just not what we could see at the time. Now she is a healer and a good one, with much more empathy for others than she might have had. Sometimes the big picture is more important than the immediate problem.

It is difficult to recognize the mind-body connection. Remember, you are what you think.

Another lady I read for is a manager for a large grocery chain with all of the related responsibility and stress. She suddenly came down with psoriasis, including all of the accompanying pain and itching. When she called, we started the "I am healing my body" therapy and I suggested she also see a skin specialist or her family doctor to verify the diagnosis. I thought maybe some new treatments might be available to ease her discomfort while we worked on the underlying cause. Part of the problem was that the rash was very visible on her face, hands, and arms. I suggested she ask the specialist to get her excused from work for a week or two to allow the rash to dissipate and be less obvious. You can't work in food with a dangerous, ugly rash obvious to all of the customers!

That was just what she wanted without being consciously aware of it—just a couple of weeks' vacation from the pressure and stress. Within two weeks the rash had disappeared and she went back to work rested and ready to face the management problem that was really troubling her. It is a well-known fact that psoriasis doesn't normally clear that quickly and will recur at will. It has been over three years with no recurrence, so apparently that attack has been cleared. I guess she is keeping it in reserve in case she needs another emergency vacation, but she continues to use the "I am" therapy for the little monthly problems, like PMS. It is amazing how well the all-purpose "I am healing my body" technique works.

We have discussed allowing herself to get too tired and stressed out by her work. She now tries to plan for and take mini-vacations more often to give her soul and her body a chance to take a break.

That's bad terminology for me. Years ago, I used this phrase often and I can still hear myself. I would say "I need a break," "Give me a break," and all variations. About fifteen years ago, the Spooks took that phrase literally and gave me a break! Not exactly what I had in mind.

I broke my left arm just below the shoulder so badly it was what the doctors called a telescoping break. The bone was broken all the way through and shoved up into the shoulder socket, cracking and breaking that socket in several places. It required nearly a year to heal and the doctors said I would never regain the use of that arm completely. I did and can do everything I did before except chin myself. (Of course, I couldn't chin myself before the break either.) You can bet, however, I don't use that phrase anymore!

Many doctors also use mind-over-matter healing techniques without being so obvious as to say, "It's all in your head." My family doctor admits there is no known cure for rheumatoid arthritis, but suggests trying various types of holistic or dietary treatments. One of his suggestions involves cherries. He swears one of his elderly patients eats cherries to control his rheumatoid arthritis. It works for him. If you think you will be helped by a specific treatment, and healing is in the cards, you probably will be! Again, mind over matter.

Stop and think about the word disease. Dis-ease. That tells the story. Your body is not at ease with some situation or problem, and if you don't understand this and get to the bottom of the problem, it may become disease, not just an uncomfortable feeling. You usually can't heal your body without uncovering and dealing with the psychological aspect behind it. Some things are as obvious as the "pain in the ass" causing a hemorrhoid, or "You make me sick" actually making you sick to your stomach. Other things are much more discrete, but remember that your soul can be very clever in pointing things out.

## *Healers: Trust Your Skills*

Another of the individuals I read for had already taken classes in massage therapy, but there was no local place to work. She worked as a secretary for the local school system and was fearful of giving that job up. The Spooks suggested that she try seeing massage clients at home on Friday night and Saturday to determine if the local people would be receptive to this form of healing.

They loved it, and in no time she had to quit working at the school in order to handle all of her clients. She sees from four to seven a day, six days a week, makes more money than she ever could have with the schools, and loves what she is doing. The Spooks say she doesn't even know who she is yet or what she will be capable of in the future. Her clients also drive a long distance to see her since this is a rural area; I've talked to some of her clients and they say her touch is "magical" and well worth the drive.

Another of the healers I've read for went to Hawaii to swim with the dolphins last year and decided to move there. She sold everything she owned, including her home, packed up all her belongings, and now lives on the Kona coast on the Big Island in Hawaii. She loves it and continues to do her healing work, teaches classes on Reiki and magnified healing, and still swims with the dolphins. This might be a little more amazing to understand and believe when you realize she is seventy-three years old. She will probably live to be over one hundred years young.

Another of the healers I've read for wants to convert the healing techniques she uses for her clients to work with horses. She is a soul who has loved and owned horses all her life. Once she called, literally in tears, because a mule she had owned for years died with his head in her lap. He had suffered a heart attack that could not have been prevented. She held his head and gave him love and comfort while he died, which took only a few minutes. She is experimenting with external herbal medications to treat sprains and injuries in horses at the present. The

Spooks say in time she will perfect this form of treatment and become famous for working with an injured racehorse in the future. I don't think the fame would matter to her, just the ability to help animals. We'll see.

Yet another healer—the one who came out to visit us to see if we were "for real" after I'd read for her and talked to her several times—has a very strong healing energy and works in many different areas. When she's come to visit she has treated various members of the family with forms of massage and healing treatments. She also works with herbal remedies and has a great knowledge of all facets of healing therapy. She is constantly studying new techniques and methods of helping people, is open to new ideas, and takes continuing education classes to up-grade her abilities. She is really special and we love having her use us as her willing guinea pigs. She was able to diagnose my son-in-law's cancer before the medical doctors did and had given him samples of the appropriate herbal medications to stop and heal the cancer. By the time he started the capsules, his condition was so badly deteriorated that he was not able to tolerate the herbs orally. As mentioned, he required daily IV treatments over a period of six weeks to finally bring the cancer under control.

All healers are not women or middle-aged. One gentlemen I read for is in his mid-eighties. He lives in Southern California with his lady friend, who is also in her eighties. He does healing and therapy work on her and others in the area. She has had open-heart surgery and he has relieved her daily pain. He also works with others doing massage therapy and using herbal supplements to help people in his senior community. He believes he maintains his own health and capabilities by helping others. He is truly amazing.

Most people in the healing services seem to have a special attitude toward other human beings. Quite often, the work they do would be too exhausting to continue if they didn't have a special calling and a desire to help other souls. Many knew all of their lives that they wanted to work in healing but time and circumstances sometimes required their patience to complete their goal.

My daughter told us she wanted to be a nurse when she was three. At that time, Rockie had a wryneck that was so stiff and painful he couldn't even hold his head up. He was in bed, trying not to move, when our three-year-old daughter raced into the room, bounced onto the bed and jumped all over, saying, "I'm going to be Daddy's nervous." She certainly was! When she was forty-one, she entered nursing school and graduated with a masters degree as a nurse practitioner at forty-eight. She graduated with many honors, and this was as a divorcee with three children. She obviously needed to complete certain karmic commitments her soul planned before obtaining her goal. She is an excellent family nurse practitioner and really is her "Daddy's nurse" now. I guess you can tell we are very proud of her. I hope she will be able to open her own clinic where both Eastern and Western medicine will be practiced. The Spooks say this will happen in time. I just wish it could be in my lifetime, but either way I'll still see it and be there.

I've heard of psychic healing, particularly in some foreign countries, in which the healers perform surgery, but leave no incisions or marks on the patient. I've never had any personal experience or read for anyone who has been healed in this manner, so I'll just have to reserve judgment. I've also heard that some of the organs removed proved during lab tests to be from some chicken or animal, so I would suggest you really investigate any such claim before you become involved.

## *Quick Remedy: One, Two, Three, Gone*

I've also heard of some people, particularly small children, being able to isolate and destroy their own cancer by the power of their own mind. When our grandchildren were young we used the "One, two, three, all gone" mental-suggestion therapy, which works extremely well with small children. They would come up crying with a new "ouchy" and ask us to stop the pain. We would just get them to put their own hand over the sore spot and repeat "One, two, three, all gone," themselves. They would, and it would quit hurting and they would run off to play more.

Small children who have not had disbelief and fear concerning health programmed into their minds yet are able to do this very successfully. By the time we become adults we have too much prejudice and fear programmed into our minds to allow us to consider how well our mind or soul can control our physical body if we will only allow it. If people would take time to consider how their thoughts make them ill, they would believe it. People are always saying "what a pain in the ass" and then end up with low back pain or hemorrhoids. People use affirmations in a negative way when they say "nothing ever goes right for me," "I'm sick and tired of . . . ," etc.

## Watch Your Language

A perfect example of how thoughts control the body occurred when we were taking a long trip with my mother, who was then in her seventies and did not want to go. We had driven for twelve hours to get to my brother's home in San Diego, with my mother complaining and unhappy all of the way. She announced, after we had been there for two hours, that it was time for us to go home. This is when I said to all present, "Mom is just being a pain in the ass," and had been all the way down.

In my great wisdom, I made that same remark repeatedly during the next five days. When we got ready to drive home I had an unbelievable case of hemorrhoids and had to sit in the middle on the bench seat of a small truck for all of the twelve-hour trip home. Speak of a pain in the ass! Boy, did I ever ask for that one and I can guarantee it is an unpleasant memory I've never forgotten. Once again, the Spooks gave me a reminder and punched holes in the "wonderfulness of myself" routine!

The funniest part is that I knew better! I had caused the problem myself and was able to clear it by myself, mostly by acknowledging my mental attitude.

## Find the Right Healer

I'm sure you all want to know how to find a good reliable healer or psychic reader because there are so many fakes out there. First, you must be open and honest with the person you are going to see. Be honest with them, and expect them to be honest with you. Then make sure they are listening to you. One of the most important parts of all types of medicine is the medical history, so give truthful answers if you honestly want help.

My mother-in-law could never find a medical doctor she liked. When I asked her if she had told him about several specific problems she was having, she replied, "No, he's the doctor, let him figure it out." How? With a crystal ball? Even that wouldn't work! I did have one prospective client who started this routine with me, including the "You're the psychic, you tell me," routine. I explained very nicely that she was wasting her money and my time if she was not open to the process or willing to be part of it. I didn't have time to play games with her. There would be no charge, but there would be no reading. When my Spooks ask for verification on a portion of the reading, I expect the client to be willing to verify or deny what they have been told. Usually I don't ask because they have already gasped out, "How did you know?" You get back what you put out and if you are not really receptive or sincerely interested in getting some honest answers, don't even get involved.

You would usually be willing to give a medical doctor the benefit of honest answers and some tests or a little time to let the treatment work. Give that same time to a healer. Most alternative treatments require a little time to work because they heal the body with a gentle nudge and will usually take a little longer. Surgery is like a hammer. It's fast and hard, but it does get results. So does the gentle nudge. It's your choice.

---

**PSYCHIC TIP: HOW TO BEGIN HEALING YOURSELF**

Here's where to start when working on your own body. Say, "I am healing . . ." and then name the portion of your own body you are working on. You can also use the "I am healing . . ." technique when you are working on someone else.

The "I am" is the part of the universal prayer and acknowledgement of who you really are. This allows the others in your soul group to lend their help when requested. You are not the little soul running around in a quandary here on earth looking for truth that you think you are. The real YOU is so much more. Try to remember that. Learn to have faith, and try to understand who you really are! And then the healing can begin.

---

### PSYCHIC TIP: RELATE HEALTH TO DEEDS

The next time you are sick or injure yourself, try to remember what you were thinking when it happened. You don't have to tell anyone, just yourself. If you're honest, you will be able to see that accidents or illnesses don't just happen—there is a relationship between thoughts and deeds.

CHAPTER EIGHT

# Psychic Games, Auras, Energy, and Prayers

Games are very useful in developing your psychic abilities. Besides the fun, you learn a great deal about your power and capabilities, as well as about other people.

## *Play the Marble Game to Find Out Where You're Headed*

Rockie and I play a meditation game with each other to see where a person's soul is at the present and where it is heading. We call it the marble game. It is a lot of fun and very revealing. To interpret, we use the colors noted in the chart on pages 118–119. You can do this with just one other person or a whole group. Young people especially like it. Here is how it is done.

Close your eyes and imagine a bag of marbles has been spilled on the floor in front of you. Pick one at random, and examine it for color and any special characteristics. Return it to the pile. Now, still with your eyes closed, look through all the marbles and pick the one you like the most. Examine it thoroughly, then replace it in the marble pile. Remember both of the marbles and all the details. Now imagine someone is handing you a ball. Examine it carefully for size, color, ribbing or markings, then throw it into the marbles and see what happens. Now open your eyes.

Ask the person what the first marble looked like and use the color chart to help determine the meaning. For instance, the marble may have been red and blue, mixed together, which might indicate they are busy enjoying life. Facing reality and truth is very important to them, either in their everyday life or in their search for greater truths. This is where they are centering right now.

Ask what the second marble looked like and again use the color chart to help determine the meaning. For instance, the second marble might be solid, shiny black, which would indicate curiosity, not hatred. Or it might be clear with blue and white swirls, which would show seeing things clearly, purity or good disposition, and the continued search for truth. It might also be bright red, if the person is heading into a very sensual time of life and the lessons needing to be learned involve the physical part of life.

Finally, ask the person to describe the ball they were handed. The bigger the ball, the bigger the ego or opinion of themselves. For instance, a basketball would indicate a very good opinion of him- or herself, maybe a little inflated. A tennis ball would be an average opinion, but also might suggest feeling a little confined because of the continuous design completely surrounding it. A jack ball would indicate low self-esteem. People who receive a ball this size could use some positive reinforcement to feel better about themselves.

When the ball is thrown into the marbles, it doesn't always scatter them as you would think! This action in your imagination shows the effect you have on other people around you—the marbles being the other people in your life. Sometimes the ball scatters them, like you do when you jump in and stir things up. Sometimes the ball bounces through, only touching one or two marbles and missing all the rest— which you do when you only touch or affect a very few people in your life. Sometimes the ball passes through the marbles and has no effect on any of them. This would suggest a person who is isolated and doesn't have any one in her life who matters that much. This could also indicate a person who feels alone, no matter how many loved ones are around her. Use your own imagination and let the Spooks fill in some of the details.

You and your friends will have fun playing the marble game. Once you know what is good and what is not, you think you can control the outcome of the game, but you can't. I've tried to pick the best marble on the table in my mind, only to have it fall out of my hand and something ugly jump into my hand instead. Others have experienced the same thing. It depends on what your attitude is and where you are centering.

## *Draw Out Your Character—and Dilemmas*

Another game to play in a group is to draw a profile of yourself. Make it just a quick sketch, not an artist's rendition. After everyone has finished, evaluate your drawings together.

If they show a lot of circular scribbles for hair, it usually indicates mental confusion, or the person is questioning the direction she is going. If the hair is too straight and severe, it can show an attitude of severity and a tendency to follow the "straight and narrow" too much. The position of the eyes indicates if the soul is looking forward and toward the future, or looking back and perhaps regretting the past. Note if they are looking upward toward the heavens and something better, or concentrating on earthbound things beneath them. If there are no eyes, the person doesn't see and doesn't want to be shown right now.

If there is no ear, the same is true: the person can't hear and doesn't want to listen. Earrings? Very interested in material things. Also note the size and position of the nose. Is it prominent, maybe too nosy and meddling? Or is it an odd shape, perhaps indicating that the nose "is out of joint" for some reason. Shoulders? If they are drawn, it may indicate a burden. Almost anything you can think of can have a psychic meaning, and nothing is drawn by accident—even when the subject swears it was an accident. We reveal our innermost feelings and problems totally unintentionally.

This is lots of fun, especially when done with a large group of people. You can also do it alone, and, once again, you can't cheat and make it all come out looking rosy, even if you try. Try it and you'll see what I mean.

## Learn to See and Read Auras

A person's aura can be quite revealing, and you can have fun learning to see and read them. Auras can also reveal more than you want to know about someone, and they can pinpoint attitudes toward life or even illness, so interpreting them can be serious business as well.

The aura, as I discussed in chapter 5, is the electromagnetic field surrounding and emanating from our bodies.

Most people can just see a little of the sparkling color around the head and shoulders of another, usually only about one or two inches wide. Some people can see the entire aura, which the Spooks say extends a little farther than you can reach in all directions and about six inches below your feet. It is a large, egg-shaped field of spinning lights and colors, changing all of the time, depending upon your physical condition and your emotional attitude at that moment.

A very good friend of mine has a doctorate in clinical psychology and social work. When we were working in the same clinic years ago, I was amazed to find out that she saw auras while she was doing counseling with her clients. She just assumed everyone did, because she had always been able to. I discovered this when she came out after a session to ask me what dark orange indicated. I told her it represented anger and aggressive behavior, which fit with his personality problems. Apparently, she had experienced great difficulty in listening to what the client was saying because she was so fascinated with watching his aura. It was pulsating in dark orange with chunks building up and falling to the floor around his chair. She was concerned that the chunks would get so deep that he wouldn't be able to leave her office, so she was happy to see him go.

My youngest son Mark, the healer, is able to see the entire aura, but he chooses not to. He was able to see when a migraine was coming on for me, twenty-four hours in advance, and he could tell when people were having pain in any particular area.

Some individuals who can see the aura choose to shut the ability off, like Mark, because of all the negative and angry things they are able to see. A person might appear to be happy and accepting a situation, while the aura shows anger and a desire to get even. One person I've heard of actually ended up in a monastery, alone most of the time, because the deceitfulness and anger of people in general was more than he could bear. He had been a minister, but standing in the pulpit, he would see so much hypocrisy that he couldn't stand it and left.

Your aura has a basic color with the other bands of color running through it. This is the portion that is usually visible around the head and shoulders and was painted by the old masters as a halo. Gold is a typical color for an aura on a individual who is reaching a higher level of soul evolvement. Green will show as the basic color in healers and pink in people who are very loving and caring. Blue indicates truth and reality. A person who normally has another color of aura may show gray and a graying of their normal color if they are depressed or not feeling well.

Rockie and I learned an easy way to see the aura years ago. I recently tried teaching this to a friend of ours who is a millwright and didn't know if he believed in paranormal phenomena or not. Within minutes he was seeing the aura of various family members, including color, size, and everything else. The psychic tip on page 152 explaiins this exercise in detail.

In general, the marble game, looking at auras, doing readings, and improving your own psychic abilities are both fun and revealing. You can improve your physical and mental health by doing these things, and you can start controlling your life much better by opening up the power of your own mind. Just be open and try it. And have fun.

## *Energy and Vibrations: A Primer*

The games above are designed to help you become aware of your energy levels, your impact on others, and how you can know things about other people that they don't tell you. Another important thing to be aware of is the affect others have on you. If you're not careful, you can find yourself drained of energy, taken advantage of, or weakened in a way you don't need to be.

Some readings are done in person out of my home, but I learned many years ago it is much easier to read over the phone. When people come to my home, sometimes they want to stay and chat for hours. Or there are distractions. One couple was deathly afraid of my big tomcat. For some unknown reason, he decided to come in and sit in the middle of the table during the reading, just looking at the two of them and purring. I think he was trying to convince them I was a witch and he was my familiar. All the time he was purring, but smiling—if cats can smile.

One morning two women were scheduled to come to my home for a reading. Just before they arrived, I suddenly started having serious chest pain and difficulty breathing. As soon as the women arrived the problem stopped. I then realized I was picking up the manner in which one woman's husband had just died. He had only been gone for a few weeks and had died quite unexpectedly from a heart attack. I was able to tell them this before the reading and reassure the woman that her husband was fine, doing well, pleased with his own progress, and on the other side.

Of course, then I got the usual "Is he in heaven or hell?" question, which still surprises me until I remember asking my psychic if my father was happy three months after his death, to which she replied he was satisfied.

## *You Pick Up Vibes All the Time*

In this instance, I was experiencing the feelings that an "empath" experiences in picking up the vibrations and feelings from another soul. We do this every day without being aware it is happening—until we return home exhausted, drained, and often angry or upset. Most people in the healing profession have to learn to clear or prevent the drain that occurs when working with and healing people.

Individuals who have very severe illnesses actually drain other people who come into the room or near them. This is not intentional; they are not aware they are doing it. You have probably experienced the exhaustion and the total drain of energy you feel when visiting a person who is dying from cancer. It is not their intention to drain your strength and they don't even know they are doing it. Just realize this is happening and mentally ask your guides to replenish your strength before you get so exhausted you have to leave. I'll give you a couple of quick, easy suggestions on how to do that later in this chapter.

Since so many people in my own family have died from cancer, we have experienced this drain first hand. My father would gain in strength and vitality when many of his children and grandchildren were visiting. He would become very animated, able to eat and converse for a long time, or at least until he had drained those visiting too much. At that point, different members of the family would decide to go back to their motels, go outside, or just take a break. As the members of the family gradually left the room, Dad would become totally exhausted and actually have to be carried back to bed to regain his strength.

I have talked to many families who have experienced the same situation with a loved one in the terminal state of cancer. It is extremely draining to the souls and bodies of all individuals involved.

Stressful situations and negative people also drain your energy. If you've ever had a minor fender bender in which no one was hurt, you know how shaken and exhausted you felt afterward. Or when you get into an argument with someone, which leaves you feeling drained and tired. Even a stressful situation at your office can have the same affect. All such things can drain your energy and strength.

## *Stop the Energy Drain*

You can replenish your aura and energy field by asking to have the universal energy replenish your strength. Just think, "I am replenishing my aura and energy field" three times and imagine a shot of energy, almost like a bolt of lightning, coming down through your head and into your body. It will work—even better than a nap. Try it the next time you feel emotionally exhausted due to stress in some situation. If you can go outside and absorb the energy and strength from nature and the universe above you, it works even better and faster.

Just be careful that you don't ask for any of these energy increases within four hours of your bedtime. I've made that mistake and found that I still have bright, shiny eyes at 3:00 AM! This is one reason I don't repeat the "I am happy, I am healthy, and I am full of energy" affirmation at night. (If for some reason you need to repeat this in the evening, try saying, "I am happy, I am healthy, and I am relaxed and at peace." Using those words will allow you to go to sleep.)

Everyone wants to know how to stop the drain from taking place, especially when dealing with sick people. Since it would be pretty selfish to stop the sick person, for example, from obtaining those few minutes of strength in order to converse—maybe for the last time—I'll explain a system that will help for a while. Just relax, close your eyes for a few moments, and imagine a white or golden light entering in through the top of your head and dispersing throughout your body. You can do this very inconspicuously in a corner of the room. You don't even have to close your eyes, but it helps in the concentration. If you can sneak off to a private spot or go outside you can raise your hands, palms up toward the sky, and imagine the same energy and strength entering into them and filling your entire body. Sometimes it helps to reinforce this with just the thought or mantra repeated three times, "I am replenishing my aura, I am replenishing my aura, I am replenishing my aura." Try it before you knock it.

If you have gone outside, try hugging a tree. Trees have fabulous amounts of energy and are happy to share it to help replenish yours. I once helped to return the favor to a beautiful big magnolia tree in our yard. The tree is very old and was very ill, losing all of its leaves and fading badly. All I did was place both hands on the tree trunk and imagine the same white or golden light coming into the tree, not into myself. I did this each day when I passed the tree. That was two years ago and we were considering having it removed before it fell onto the house. You should see it now. It is big, beautiful, and shining. It was crying for help and the Spooks assisted in helping it. The Law of Return: what you take, you must replace. Try it. It's fun and very rewarding.

Keep in mind, some individuals can be very selfish, fully aware that they are draining you, and they don't care. If you sense this is happening, just imagine a large pair of scissors in your hand and imagine cutting the psychic drain they have plugged into your head. While you do this, say "I am stopping the energy drain," three times and it will be stopped. Quite often the person who was deliberately "sucking your strength" will get a puzzled look on his face and leave the area. They may not say anything, but they got the message! Some individuals will even say, "Boy, you really zapped me." Remember—no sympathy for them. Cut them off.

## *Clean Up Your Aura*

When I am reading for individuals who are experiencing very traumatic or emotional situations, I often recommend that they take a shower to wash off their aura to get rid of the negative vibrations they have accumulated. When you are visiting a very sick person in the hospital, you are being drained by their need for help, drained by your anger at the lack of care being given, and drained by your inability to do anything to really help, or sometimes you meet a person having a tough time in any number of ways and find yourself drained for similar reasons. These feelings and frustrations accumulate as a dark substance on your aura.

To clean your aura, you need to stand under the shower, let the water run from the top of your head on down for three minutes to completely wash it. It doesn't matter if you wear a shower cap to protect your hairdo, just let water pass over your entire body for three minutes. You can consciously think of cleaning your aura or not. It doesn't matter. It just works.

One lady I read for had been at the hospital helping to care for her mother who had just had a very serious operation. She came home totally exhausted and called. I recommended she take the aura-cleansing shower, to which she replied, "I'm just too tired." The Spooks finally talked her into it, instead of just falling into bed. She called the next night and admitted she had showered against her better judgment, but that it had helped tremendously. She slept well, rested better, and awoke refreshed.

Smog and gray smoke in many large cities is an accumulation of negative energy from not only the pollution but the pain, anger, and frustration experienced by the souls living there. Long ago, Rockie and I got in the habit of calling these negative energy forces gumbas. We do it to this day, forgetting that others may not know what a gumba is. It is a negative energy force but can be cleansed and removed by just plain old water. This is probably why everything looks brighter and feels better after a rainstorm. It does more than just clear the air. Try it the next time you feel angry, tired, frustrated, and any of the other exhausting emotions we experience every day. A shower does more than just cleanse the body. It also cleans the soul.

## Cleanse a Room with Salt

Another way to cleanse and lift the negatives off of a room, area, person, animal, or any animate or inanimate object involves using just plain old table salt. Some psychics and healers insist you need to use sea salt, but we have found plain table salt is just as effective.

You may have heard of "saging" a room. It involves burning some form of sage or other incense or fragrance in a room to remove evil or negative vibrations. I don't believe in evil or satanic forces, but I do believe in negative vibrations or thought forms. Quite often, we create the negative vibrations, just from our own anger and thoughts, and we can help to clear them with the salt sprinkled (just a few grains) in each corner of a room. Don't use enough so anyone will notice, but you will notice by the change in attitudes of those in the room or the general feeling in the room after the salt therapy.

The problem with saging or burning incense or candles is that it becomes too obvious and will probably have to be explained. In some situations you just don't want to explain to a person who doesn't want to hear. Salt is quiet, clean and has no smell. Try it.

## For Safety's Sake: White Light

For years we put what we refer to as the white light around a vehicle one of our children or grandchildren was driving or riding in. I don't know if it really works, but no one has died in a car accident yet. A recent experience one of our grandsons had was really pretty funny. He was coming home from work when the person in front of him suddenly stopped. He was not able to stop in time and hit the other person's bumper. The other driver jumped out and ran away. I've heard of hit and run, but never this variation. The police decided the driver had probably stolen the vehicle or had drugs or alcohol in his possession, and they did not issue a citation to our grandson. Weird. I'm sure the Spooks had something to do with this, and the white light was in effect.

We have also imagined the white light completely enveloping the entire house to give protection to the individuals inside. You just imagine it as a big clear canopy like a dome you might see in outer space movies. You can place a white light around any object or person you want protected just by thinking of it.

You can place this white protective light over an object or person. Just ask your Spooks to envelope the item in the white protective light and imagine it being there.

## *Employ the Power of Prayer*

This brings up the idea of prayer, which people define many different ways. Some, for example, simply want to talk to deceased relatives. To accomplish that, I suggest simply that you try "thinking" of talking to the relatives you want to reach. This, incidentally, is also a method you can use to contact your own guides or protective Spooks.

Note that this is not praying in the usual sense of the word. It's more like a normal conversation between two people. Just imagine what you would like to say if the person were standing right in front of you. You don't have to say anything out loud, so no one will walk by and think you've gone nuts! You are sending communication by telepathic means. Just think it!

You have probably read or heard about the "bush telegraph" in Australia between the aborigines. People can be separated by an entire continent and know the message someone is sending. Distance doesn't matter. The same is true of those on the other side. The other side is as close as two feet in front of you. It is a different dimension and different plane, but it's as close as you want it to be. When you believe that, you don't have to yell, get a long-distance call, or anything else. You are already in the same space or area. Better yet, you don't have to say it. Thinking the message sends it on its way.

Those on the other side can only hear or understand what you want to send to them. They have bigger and better things to do than eavesdropping on our constant babbling thoughts or conversations. By comparison to the clear, precise thoughts and messages sent to each other on the other side, we really do babble.

My family of origin was Catholic, had rosaries, went to mass, and had Catholic funerals. I was taught how to pray to specific saints as a child, but it never made much sense to me then or now, so I don't. If praying in that fashion gives you comfort, however, continue praying in that way. I just recommend cutting out the middleman. Go directly to the source. For instance, I would say "Mom, I need your help with [subject, person, or problem]. See if you can do something about [whatever]!"

KISS. Keep It Simple, Stupid! Don't repeat the problem over and over. Just because the person on the other side is dead doesn't mean they have become deaf or stupid! Once is enough. I might be just as likely to say, "God, please help me with [whatever]." Or I might just say, "Hey Spooks, whoever is free right now, I need help with [whatever]." Believe me, informal is best. Remember, they are your family and friends. It may seem too easy, but it works just as well.

Most of the well-known prayers, like the Lord's Prayer or the Twenty-third Psalm, are often not listened to or understood by the person repeating them. It is just something you remember from being a child and perhaps at a more innocent age, so it gives you comfort. If it makes you feel good, do it. If it makes you uncomfortable, don't. Make up your own prayer. Say what is right for you at the moment. I'm sure most of you can remember making up additional verses to the old-fashioned "Now I Lay Me Down To Sleep" prayer you were taught when a small child. I'm also sure you can remember that most of them weren't very reverent either. I'm sure if you have a runaway truck bearing down on you, you don't think of or have time to say the entire Lord's Prayer. You are much more likely to think or say "God help me!" or something obscene. Try being real.

## *Visualize to Change Your Situation*

How do we go about changing things in our lives that we really want to change? I always remind people I'm reading for that, "God helps those who help themselves." You have to be willing to assume responsibility for where you are now and where you want to go. This requires a lot of honesty on your part, and you have to be part of the process. You can't just say, "Well, I asked God for a million dollars and he didn't send it to me, so I don't believe any of that mumbo jumbo."

First, if you asked for a million dollars, go back and read the part of this book on karma. You can only receive what you have coming to you karmically. When you receive a large amount of money, it always changes your life style completely. Any person who has ever won the lottery had it coming to them on a karmic basis or they wouldn't have won.

And maybe you do, as well. At the very least, you can bring prosperity or changes into your life. First, make your desire known to your guides. Then envision yourself in the new situation that would be part of this new life.

For example, say you really need and want a different job. Imagine yourself in a new job situation, new office, with new people around you. Envision everyone smiling and happy. Envision yourself as being happy and relating to the others around you. Imagine how good it feels to go to work in the morning. Think of liking the new job so much you aren't clock watching. It's fun to be there and you are feeling appreciated and happy with the new situation. See yourself receiving your paycheck and being pleasantly surprised by the amount of money you are paid. Ask to see yourself several years later, still happy in that new job.

Don't do this just once. Add to the plan each day and continue to embroider the details. The more you can visualize, the more you will actually receive. Remember the plan, believe it, and start living like it is going to happen.

You can also use the "I am" affirmation (see chapter 6) in working on changing your situation. Say, "I am being offered a new job," "I am happy with the new job offered," or whatever you want. Then get to work: Write a new resume and fill out job applications. You can't sit at home, just saying positive affirmations and doing nothing to help yourself. Again: "God helps those who help themselves." You have to do your part. You can just improve the responses to your actions.

Note: Don't ask for another's person job. You can ask for a job like that person's, but not that specific job. That would be asking the guides or Spooks to take something away from another person and give it to you. They cannot and will not do that, so don't ask for it! Besides, there is more than enough to go around. You can have something similar, so plan to get it.

And remember to be careful what you ask for, because you might get it! Make sure you know all of the positive and negative sides of what you are asking for. Don't make it just a fantasy you might like to have without knowing how much might really be involved.

Do you really know how much time that job will require? How much education you will need? In other words, don't ask to be a neurosurgeon unless you are willing to spend many years in school getting educated to the point that position would require.

When I was forty years old, all of our children left home in the same year and I seriously considered going back to school. If I had, it would have been to become a doctor. But I was honest enough with myself to admit that I didn't want to work that hard! Because of other circumstances, I probably wouldn't have been able to complete the educational requirements anyway, but at least I admitted the truth at that moment to myself. Don't run around blaming everyone else for not being able to return to school when in truth you really didn't want to. Besides, if I had returned to school I wouldn't have continued my involvement with the psychic field, so I'm sure I made the right choice.

The same would be true with almost anything you really wanted. A new home, almost any physical thing you can think of. You want a new location or a new city to live in? Just picture it and start programming the change. I've even heard of some people who have placed maps or pictures of what they wanted in conspicuous places, like on the refrigerator, the mirror in the bathroom, or a new keychain hanging in the car. You can have almost anything you want, if you are willing to do your part too. You can't say "God, I want a new car," and then sit and wait. It doesn't work that way. God helps those . . .

## It's Not About the Material World

Be careful when you are asking for material things. We get so involved with material things in this world, we sometime lose track of the fact that they are just "things," things that can distract you from the things that are really important. Years ago, Rockie and I got a motor home. It was really neat, and everyone in the family loved it. We all went on camping trips together, took long trips on the freeways, taking turns driving, and just in general had a good time. The problem is, we got to loving the motor home itself, and not the fun we were having in it. The Spooks were happy to point it out.

The first problem involved the top on the passenger side of the vehicle. It swiped a street sign and put a nice little "can opener" mark in the skins one inch wide and two feet long. No big deal, we thought, until we found out they had to remove all of the siding beneath and around the area to replace and repair it from the bottom up. Oops! It meant much more money and time involved in the repair than we had expected.

But we hadn't gotten the message. After about six things happened to the motor home—among other things, a tree limb crunched the air conditioner on the roof, thieves broke in and stole the CB radio and stereo system, and the engine caught on fire—we figured it all out. Don't love it, or you'll lose it. We could like it, have fun in it, but once we got emotional about every little fender bender, the Spooks stepped in by increasing the damage until we figured it out. The accidents stopped.

## *Harness Soul Power*

The power of many souls working together could completely change the direction the world is taking if enough individuals would be willing to try to work toward the same goal. Many years ago, people were involved in something called the Harmonic Convergence, but I don't think enough people really tried or took it seriously enough. Various others have tried similar prayers for peace or help for the physical earth. It might be totally amazing if enough of us tried hard enough. I'd like to live to see that and would be happy to be involved. Remember the old saying, "Faith can move mountains." I think we actually could.

Occasionally you will hear or read about some fantastic feat of strength by one single individual lifting an automobile off of another person. No one can explain where that type of strength or power comes from, and a shot of adrenalin just isn't enough to explain it. Superman, super-human strength, love, wisdom, power, and all of the superlatives you can imagine don't explain it. Think what mankind could do if we could harness this and use it for the good of all.

---

**PSYCHIC TIP: TEACH YOURSELF TO SEE AURAS**

Find a person who is willing to let you look at their aura. Have him or her stand in front of a blank white or off-white wall. Ask the person to take several big breaths, think of something pleasant, and relax. Sit in front of them, six to ten feet away, and stare at the spot just between their eyes (the location of the third eye). Try not to blink. After just a minute or so you will start to see something almost like a vibrating heat wave surrounding the head and shoulders. Don't take your eyes off of the forehead, but be aware of what is developing in your peripheral vision. You may actually see a color or you may only sense what the color is.

You'll probably end up in a giggling mess, but it does work. When you become accustomed to looking at an aura, it will be much easier. Keep in mind that if you go around looking at auras without permission, you may get some surprises. Auras are very personal and people may not be what you thought they were.

In fact, it is unethical to try to read an aura unasked. Since it is unethical, your Spooks may decide to have fun with you and show you something that you didn't expect, or exaggerate something you expected to learn about the other person. Leave it alone. In some situations, reading an aura can be like trying to read someone else's mail or eavesdrop on a phone call. If you don't want it done to you, then don't do it. Remember, "Do unto others as you would have them do unto you!"

---

### PSYCHIC TIP: PRACTICE PROGRAMMING
### OR PRAYING FOR SOMETHING

You can confirm the power of prayer or visualization easily. Start out with something little like a phone call or a letter from someone you would like to hear from. Just say you need an answer to some question you had previously posed. Just don't laugh at people when they call and don't know exactly why!

---

### PSYCHIC TIP: BUILD YOUR PSYCHIC STRENGTH
### BY MANIPULATING CLOUDS

You can increase or decrease the size of clouds just by looking at them and thinking of changing the size, shape, or color. Years ago, I taught one of my grandsons to do this as an entertainment on a long automobile trip. He was fascinated and proved to be extremely adept at this ability. Just pick a cloud, a very small wisp to start with and start sending the message that it is getting smaller and smaller. Continue to concentrate, and it will actually disappear and dissolve right in front of your eyes! Don't pick the biggest thunderhead in the sky. Start small.

This is a quick, easy thing to learn and will really help to convince you of your own abilities. After you have found you can make a cloud disappear just through the power of your own mind, and have proven it to a few others, you will have more confidence in yourself as a capable, intelligent soul and be able to take on some of the bigger problems confronting you.

By the way, my grandson can now dissolve or create clouds at will. Maybe this is part of what the old-fashioned rainmakers were really all about!

CHAPTER NINE

# Readings and Results

Periodically, the Spooks remind me, through a reading, of the old saying, "I cried because I had no shoes until I met a man who had no feet." Some of the people who have been calling me for years have had a series of tragedies in their lives that would totally overwhelm most of us, yet they are still able to laugh, love, and learn. These are really remarkable souls.

## *The Silver Lining in All Tragedies*

I have been doing readings for Ann, who has faced many trials, for at least ten years. When she first called me it was regarding her worry, fear, and concern for her three-year-old child, who had just lost his foot in an automobile accident (see chapter 2). Doctors, you'll recall, had tried desperately to save the foot and the child nearly died from infections before the decision to amputate was made. Ann was five months pregnant with her third child at the time and had a seventeen-year-old son—who had been driving when the accident occurred. He was not at fault, however.

Ann worked part time for the city, and had just bought a flower shop. She financed it with loans against her home and she feared losing everything. Yet she was much more upset about the loss of her son's foot than he was. He has since proven he can do anything the other boys can do. It wasn't going to stop him!

Ann gave birth to her third child with no complications, as predicted, and the little girl, now five, is really a joy for the family. Ann's business survived and is doing so well she is planning on expanding. The Spooks say she will double the business volume before long.

Every tragedy in your life has a purpose, the Spooks say, and it's always constructive in some way, even if it doesn't seem that way. Ann's husband was involved in a very serious automobile accident not long ago. He is slowly recovering from the surgeries now, but he is still disabled and needs a cane to walk. There is the possibility of more surgery on his hip. The only good part of this particular experience is that being an employee when the accident occurred gave him the insurance and worker's compensation benefits he would not have had as a self-employed individual. He had really wanted to start his own business, which had not been possible. Ann felt that if this disability had to happen, and was something her husband had to experience in order to learn, at least the financial burden was not as great as it might have been.

The other benefit received during this recovery period is the fact that they have found time to really communicate with each other, set new goals for the future, and improve their personal relationship.

The other near-tragedy that occurred in Ann's life was her older son's attempted suicide. He had felt guilty and responsible for years over the loss of his brother's foot. This guilt, along with school and peer pressures, brought the whole problem to a head. He is in counseling now and letting go of the accumulated guilt and anger.

The amazing thing is Ann's attitude. She doesn't say "poor me," has a good sense of humor, and can see the possible positive side of each of these misfortunes. It has really been a struggle to juggle all of the emotional and financial burdens she has handled and she never gives up.

One of her favorite quips is, "Cheer up, things could be worse. So, I cheered up and sure enough—they got worse." With her, I don't know whether to laugh or cry. The Spooks agree, but she is doing a fantastic job with the karmic situation she has chosen.

## *Looking for Love . . . and Finding It*

The question most often asked during a reading is, "Will I find some-one to love, who will love me?" Everyone is looking for that special someone to share their life with, that one person they can really com-municate with. Some have waited so long and lost so often they just don't believe it will ever happen for them.

One woman, Sherry, was referred to me by another psychic about five years ago. The other psychic had been talking to her for quite a long time, and felt input from another source might be helpful. Besides, some of my clients like to get another opinion or verification to see if we are seeing the same future for them. The astounding thing is that very often we do! I've seen as many as five identical readings from five different sources, and the psychics don't even know each other.

In reading for Sherry over a period of two years, I always saw the same thing. Sherry was in her mid-thirties, had never been married, but had been engaged twice. Both of those engagements were broken when her fiancés were killed in accidents. She was very pretty, intel-ligent, and had no problem dating, but she couldn't find that special someone and had gotten to the point where she was afraid to look.

In addition, she was a speech therapist who really loved children, but she was deathly afraid of childbirth. This, it turned out, had karmic origins. The Spooks said she had lived on the prairies as a farm wife in a past life and had spent most of her adult life pregnant. She had lost most of her children as babies.

In the first readings, the cards said she would marry at thirty-seven years of age to a widower with two children. During the next couple of years the details continued to fill in—and Sherry was a stickler for details. The man was not available for marriage at the present, because his wife was still alive, but she had a terminal illness. He would have a fourteen-year-old son and a twelve-year-old daughter who would look just like Sherry. There would be no serious problems; the children would accept her almost instantly as their mother and she would feel they were really her own children.

The man was really a good person. A complete physical description gradually emerged, including a funny nose that had been broken when he was younger. When they met it would be through a dark-haired, female friend in a city north of where Sherry lived. Sounds like what you'd hear from a gypsy fortune teller in a "too good to be true" routine, right? Sometimes I doubted what the Spooks were having me tell her, because it sounded too perfect. Too much as if it was being created exactly for her. Well, it was.

One day, Sherry called me, bubbling over with excitement. She had just met the man, exactly in the manner predicted. She had never really believed the whole prediction either, but had continued to call me just to work on her daily problems of work, dates, etc.

She had been invited for a weekend to visit a dark-haired friend who lived in a town fifty miles north of her. When she arrived they mentioned they were going to have a few neighbors over that afternoon for a barbecue. One of the neighbors was Bill, a tall dark-haired man with a funny nose, whose wife had just died from a brain tumor the previous November. The wife had gradually deteriorated over the past three years while they tried every means of saving her. He had two children, a boy and a girl. Sherry and Bill felt an immediate rapport and made plans to meet the following weekend. Sherry couldn't believe what was happening and neither could Bill. He had not even considered dating up to this point, since his wife's illness and death had been so recent. And the children were just as predicted. The picture of Bill's daughter could have been Sherry at the age of twelve.

Bill was a very considerate, thoughtful person who constantly amazed Sherry. She kept waiting for the other shoe to drop, as no one she had ever known was that sincere and honest. She called me repeatedly when they first started dating and couldn't believe it when he proposed in less than one month. Bill suggested the house could be redecorated or they could buy a new one, the choice was up to Sherry. After Bill's daughter confided in her one day, Sherry realized he was being overly concerned for her feelings. Apparently, he had put all of his deceased wife's pictures away and asked his children not to discuss how they missed their mother with Sherry. He didn't want her to feel bad. Sherry explained that she wanted them to talk openly about their mother. There weren't any feelings of jealously or resentment toward the woman who had been Bill's wife.

Instead, a feeling of love and friendship was present, almost as if she and the dead woman were sisters. She felt approval and a blessing from the other side. Sherry said, "It's like my sister gave birth to these children for both of us. Like we've known all along we would share raising them. It's crazy, but that's how I feel." The pictures came back out.

They were married in October that same year and only waited until October so a big church wedding could be arranged with both families present. Sherry's stepchildren are the same age as all of her nieces and nephews, and the cousins all resemble each other. Sherry had never dreamed all of this could happen, even when the Spooks kept saying it would.

Sherry still would not want to give birth to a baby. That's fine with Bill, who doesn't want any more children either. She has her children and says she is so lucky with her perfect, made-to-order family.

I have also been reading for Sherry's best friend, Kay, who keeps me posted on her own situation as well as Sherry's. Kay's future is just as certain as Sherry's was. The fantastic man foreseen as her future husband turned up in her life, as predicted, about six months after Sherry's wedding. Truly, it was a storybook romance complete with roses and love poems. When predicted, it sounded like something out of a romance novel, but Kay has really earned this love. They have been together in several past lives, think together, and act together. They did marry, but with roses come some thorns, which have been provided by a very immature son from a previous marriage. The Spooks say it will all work out, but not until the son gets a little older and wiser.

## When It's Time to Part, Act

The first time Sharon ever called me was about twelve years ago. She was returning from a business conference for city employees, had stopped to visit a friend and got my number. The first thing the Spooks gave me was her intense desire to end a twenty-five-year marriage. She was extremely unhappy and so was her husband, but neither wanted to be the "bad guy." It had been one of those "we must stay together for the children's sake" situations. The children were grown, but they just didn't know what to do next. The Spooks told her to start the divorce immediately so they could both get on with their lives. They were stagnating in their current situation and both needed to move forward. The guides also said he wanted a new start as much as she did.

Sharon filed for the divorce and her husband immediately agreed with her. He moved out and she felt better than she had in years. Now she was ready for a more challenging career.

The Spooks gave the information as to where to go and what the first step should be. It turned out exactly as predicted and during a later call she was very concerned because a group of people wanted her to run for the City Council. This was not a tiny town, but one of the satellite cities surrounding one of the big metropolitan cities. She had worked for the city but had never considered entering into politics. The Spooks said, "Go for it. You'll win and it's just a beginning." She is now the mayor of a large city in Southern California and a group wants her to run for a state office. Guess what the Spooks said? That's right, same message, "Go for it." She can go as high and far as she wishes, but she would never have tried had she stayed in the unhappy marriage situation. Her children are proud of her accomplishments, but her ex-husband is a little embarrassed in having his ex-wife as the mayor and would have discouraged her from ever running for office in the first place. He feels it makes him look stupid for letting her get away. He has also remarried and is very happy in that relationship.

Sharon enjoys her work, believes in the concepts set forth in this book and intends to remain honest throughout her political career. You can just guess what her most serious problem is. That's right, "When will I find someone I can love?"

Since I have so many of them, I've devoted the whole next chapter to love stories.

## Karma Works in Mysterious Ways

I have known Ellen and her family for a long time, and started doing readings for Ellen when she was around eighteen. She made a mistake at sixteen, had an abortion without discussing her intentions with any-one, and discovered ten years later that she would never be able to have children. Her older sister had the same physical problem and had finally given up ever being able to have children after fifteen years of marriage. She had gone through many tests and a great deal of medical expense only to be disappointed with the repeated diagnosis.

When Ellen told me the diagnosis, the Spooks said it was wrong, she would have three children as predicted. She laughed and said "Lots of luck." When she was about twenty-nine years old, she called one evening for a reading, after just going through a divorce and break-ing up with a new "Mr. Wonderful." In the process of the reading, the Spooks warned her to be careful. She could get pregnant; the cards also indicated a child. I hadn't heard anything from her for over a year when I got a slightly frantic call from her mother. Ellen had just given birth to a perfectly normal, healthy little girl, wasn't married and was considering putting the child up for adoption. Could her childless sis-ter adopt the baby? Would it hurt the family?

Ellen truly loved her older sister, but didn't know if she would be able to stand seeing the child growing up. Maybe an outside adoption would help the memories to fade gradually. The Spooks wanted me to tell her she would never be able to forget anyway; memories of the baby would always be there. With her sister raising the baby, she could see her as the aunt, know she was loved and well cared for. Besides, Ellen would marry again and have two more children as originally pre-dicted. All three children would be near each other and be raised to-gether. She ended up realizing that she had been chosen as a surrogate or proxy mother for her sister. She laughed, and thought the situation was strange because she would have offered to carry a child for her sister. Neither ever considered this a possibility because both believed Ellen could not carry a child full term.

Ellen could see this as a gift of love for her sister, even if not origi-nally intended. When I last talked to Ellen, she had remarried and has had her other two children, a son and a daughter. She and her sister live in the same town, babysit for each other and visit constantly. They will tell the baby girl the whole story when she grows up, but for the present time, Ellen is just "Aunty," proud of her choice and herself when she sees her sister's happiness. And she really loves her little "niece."

Sometimes changing a person's perspective on a situation completely changes the options available and the direction a person will choose to take. Ellen wanted to let her sister adopt the baby, but feared what her feelings in the future might be. Guidance from the other side made accepting the situation much easier. She was also comforted in knowing she would have two more children in the future. Ellen is happy with her decision and can see so much good coming out of what appeared to be a tragedy. Now she says, "We all won!"

## You Can't Escape Karma

Remember my older brother who always moved to escape from the ever-present noise of motorcycles? Well, every time he got ready to make a move, and there had been six in a period of twelve years, he and his wife called for a reading. The Spooks always told them when their house would sell, the price, and some information on the buyer. It was uncanny, but it worked every time.

In one of the later moves, they weren't haunted by motorcycles. This time it was chainsaws cutting down the forest next to his home, and terrible wind storms uprooting huge, old pine trees on his land. The noise didn't bother him as much as the loss of the trees. (This man had been known to plant ninety trees on a one-half acre plot of land!) My brother said they just wanted to be protected by trees, not buried under them!

Once, my sister-in-law wanted to know if my brother would be happy in their new home in Paradise, California. The Spooks said "If he doesn't like Paradise, he wouldn't like the Garden of Eden, either." I think the message was pretty clear and they had no motorcycles or chainsaws bothering them in Paradise.

They moved again, but this time because he had terminal cancer and the move brought his wife closer to her children. This is the brother I mentioned before who made all of the arrangements and took care of everything prior to leaving—the one who left a legacy I'll never live up to. I guess you can tell I'm kind of proud of him.

After my brother died, his wife fought a round with cancer and won. She also married the man I had predicted would come into her life. When she met him she called to say that she thought I had been full of it and just trying to make her feel better. He was everything that had been predicted. They married five years ago and are very happy.

## Money Sometimes Comes from Unexpected Places

Another couple I've read for was told by the Spooks that the money they needed for a down payment on a home would be provided in two months by a dark-haired man. I tried to get more information, but the only answer was that it was related to the wife and was a gift.

Two months later, they called to let me know the very unusual source of the money. The wife had been married for a very short time several years before to a young man who had recently been killed in an automobile accident. He had never remarried and had continued to carry his ex-wife as the beneficiary on his life insurance policy. She told his parents and sister that she couldn't accept the money, but they insisted. He had recently mentioned that she was still his beneficiary and he wanted it that way. He had discussed it with his family only two weeks before his death. He told his family that he felt guilty about the divorce; he was so young at the time and hadn't really tried, and now it was too late. It was truly a gift from beyond the grave and from a totally unexpected source, but definitely related to the wife.

How did the subject of the insurance come up, just before he died in a totally unexpected automobile accident? Who arranged this conversation so there would be no question about his beneficiary being an ex-wife he hadn't seen or spoken to in years? These are some of the inexplicable things that happen all the time. Since this was definitely his wish, the wife thanked him sincerely for his help and concern for her from the other side.

## In Love, Age Doesn't Matter

Age is apparently no factor in those interested in having a reading, as I found much to my surprise. Probably the oldest caller I've had was a woman who admitted to being eighty-three years old. Her concern was what her husband's reaction was going to be when he got out of jail and found out she and her boyfriend had sold his pickup truck and spent the money! At first I thought someone was just pulling my leg, but it turned out to be genuine. Mary was eighty-three years old, liked to dance and party, and had been married for the past seven years to a man ten years younger. When he got into trouble with drunk driving, resisting arrest, and assaulting a police officer, she was perfectly happy to see him jailed and out of her life. The only thing unexpected was that he was being released early due to health problems and her main problem was coming home from jail.

Mary had filed for a divorce and expected the divorce to be finalized before her husband was released. The Spooks recommended that she make a settlement through her lawyer real fast and then go visit someone in another state until her ex had time to cool off.

The next question was, "Will I find someone to marry who likes to dance and have fun but isn't an alcoholic?" Totally unbelievable: eighty-three, five marriages, numerous boyfriends, dancing—and looking for a sixth husband! With her attitude and zest for life she'll probably live to 120 if an angry husband or jealous wife doesn't catch up with her first.

## *Leave Another Without Anger*

We walk with and beside another soul for a period of time. It might be weeks, years, or a lifetime, but only as long as you are each working on your own karmic situations, as long as your soul is still growing and learning. When the time is complete, the best scenario is to part with no anger or hatred and continue in the learning process for your own souls. The problem is that in the physical plane, we carry all the emotional baggage we are trying to learn from to let go of a losing relationship. That is part of the reason we sometimes get involved in ugly divorces.

I have worked with and counseled some individuals through these ugly divorces with all of the typical problems, short of murder. People just can't believe they will ever be able to tolerate that blankety blank ever again in their lives. They will teach him or her! It takes time, but they are always surprised that time really does heal all wounds. I try to remind them that they are never really clear when children and custody are involved. It may be years down the road, but you will have to see each other at a graduation, marriage, or the birth of a grandchild. Keep that in mind when you are making the "never again" threats. You will want to make life easier for your children and grandchildren in the future. You may never forget, but time eases the pain almost to the point of becoming funny in some cases.

I read once for a man whose wife actually moved out of the house with all of the furnishings, including a freezer full of food and two children before the husband got home from work. This was after she had been involved in an extra-marital affair which he forgave and was helping to raise the baby. It was an ugly divorce that went on for a number of years. Years later, the husband attended his niece's wedding with both wives. He danced with both, and introduced them as his first wife and his current wife! If I hadn't been at the wedding, I wouldn't have believed it. Kind of made you wonder what he had in mind for the future of his current marriage, but they are still happily married. He and his first wife really buried the hatchet—and not in each other's skull. Just as strange was the fact that the two wives really liked each other. I can remember trying to convince him that time would really change how he felt and reacted to the tragedy, but at the time he was experiencing the mess, he couldn't believe it.

## Men Are Sensitive Souls

Don't think only women call for readings. I have a large group of men calling also. Their concerns aren't that different; the need for love and success is equal for men and women. Remember, we incarnate as male and female in different lifetimes to learn all the aspects of love, life, and emotions. If we were allowed to only incarnate into one sex or the other, we would become too set in our ways and with our attitudes, so we need to try on the glass slippers as well as the moccasins.

One of the most unusual, unexpected situations that comes up in reading for men is realizing that many of them really don't like the macho, sex-machine image that society has created for them. I am told by men "I get so tired of being expected to perform, just because I'm a man. Women expect us to make a pass, expect us to be willing and ready for any sexual encounter at the drop of a hat. Some guys act that way because they think they are supposed to, but most of us really don't feel that way." Are you listening, ladies?

Contrary to popular belief, most men still find the girl who says "No" a special find—someone who doesn't jump into every bed in town, a woman who realizes sex is related to love and shouldn't just be thrown away. Another thing I'm finding in my readings is that morals are improving, the good old free-love group is dwindling down, and people are beginning to realize that nothing is free. Perhaps it is because of AIDS, herpes, and the upswing of VD, but I believe another important factor is that sex without love and emotion is pretty empty.

Quite a few of my calls also come from the gay community, both male and female. Their feelings, needs, and desires are so similar to the heterosexual population that it is unbelievable. About the only difference I've been able to see is who walks into the bedroom with them before the door is closed, and the stigma placed on the entire group by society. Granted, some people in the gay community are only looking for sex and a good time, but the same is true in "straight" society. Most of the people who call me sincerely want a long-term relationship. A real loving, caring, communication situation, equivalent to marriage. And some have just that.

Several female couples I read for have been together for over twenty-five years, own property together, live together, travel, and share their happiness and sorrow. They are more secure than many marriages because there are no legal documents forcing them to continue in the relationship. They want to be together.

One outstanding soul I have read for in the gay community is an example of family caring and love for everyone. I've known her and read for her for years and I am constantly surprised by her kindness and willingness to help others, particularly her family. She comes from a large family, has mostly sisters, and was devastated by her father's death a number of years ago. The whole family was worried about what to do with the elderly mother. She refused to live with some of her married daughters or their families, and was still too healthy to be put into a retirement home, something she couldn't afford anyway.

My client decided she would use her good credit rating, if her mother could help with the down payment and buy a mobile home for the two of them and one of the other sisters who was also gay. They carried out this plan, and the home was much nicer than the apartment my friend had been used to. Maria and her sister shared the house payments, and it cost her a little more per month than the apartment, but it was worth the difference. The mother had the master bedroom, and the sister took the other large bedroom. That left Maria with the smallest bedroom and the largest share of the responsibility and expense. She never complained about the arrangement because it was for "Mom."

Last year, her mother died very unexpectedly from a heart attack while Maria was at work. Maria was the one to find her when she came home. It was very traumatic, so much so that she didn't even consider moving into the master bedroom until almost a year later. This was still hallowed ground and could not be used until the possibility of having a room mate to help with expenses arose. At this time, Maria decided maybe she could move her things into the master bedroom so she would have access to the shower and bath. A big hubbub arose in the family regarding the mother's bedroom set, as everyone had an opinion on the use, sale, etc.

Maria called me to see what the Spooks said. The message from her mom was very clear. She wanted Maria to keep the bedroom set as an inheritance from her. It didn't matter what anyone else said or thought. The rest of her message to Maria was that she understood her lifestyle and had no negative feelings about her possibly sharing the bed with a future girlfriend or husband. It didn't matter.

Maria gently whispered that this is what had really bothered her. She thought it might be dishonoring her mother or her parents, not showing the proper respect, if she slept in their bed. That's why she had considered selling the entire bedroom set. The Spooks said, "No, it is a gift from your mother. It is her way of saying she really understands. It is her thanks to you for providing her with a home and security after your father died."

Maria said her mother had always said she understood and had no unhappy feelings about her lifestyle. She just had a funny feeling that she couldn't put into words, until the Spooks did it for her. She verified that this had been her deepest concern. It was a matter of respect for her parents. She has come a long way and, gay or straight, she is someone I'm proud to know.

## *Your Gender: Your Choice*

The Spooks tell us that in some cases a soul will choose to incarnate as one sex only until they are strongly encouraged by souls with more wisdom to accept the opposite sex role to balance the learning process. The learning process requires that we understand the physical life from the viewpoint of each sex due to the social attitudes in our society. In the first incarnation as a man, the soul who has always incarnated as a female may still have all the typical female attitudes, feelings, desires, and actions, but is stuck in a man's body. The mannerism, body language, and behavior may be female, but the new body is male. The only physical body that attracts them is the one they've always been attracted to, a man's. You can often see the transition problem in small children, very strong tomboy girls, and very effeminate boys. Some souls can't make the change in just one lifetime or they are too stubborn to accept the new role.

## *Watch Your Attitudes*

Some individuals choose the life described above, and others are forced into it because of attitudes and behavior in a previous life. When I see and hear of groups who are going out of their way to make life miserable and unhappy for the homosexual population, I can't help but wonder how they will like wearing that pair of shoes next time. One man I read for was very homophobic. He really had a problem with gay men, and went out of his way to make remarks and increase the prejudice against them. Imagine his shock and pain to discover his oldest son was gay and had known it since he was a small child. This very macho man, into hunting, fishing, all of the very masculine sports, had a gay son. He was suicidal and felt he couldn't live with the shame. With the help of the Spooks and some education on life in the gay community, he was able to accept his son and his son's lifetime partner who was, you guessed it, a real nice guy.

You reap what you sow, so take a serious look at any of your prejudices. Not only against the sexual preference of individuals, but also against other races and religions. Any situation that can cause anger, hatred, or any strong, emotional feeling is probably of karmic origin. You may have difficulty in changing your innermost feelings, but be very careful of what you say or do. If you put yourself into the other person's position and imagine how it would feel, you'll think twice before you act.

If you sincerely try to change your behavior, a little every day, and try not to be the one who throws the first stone, you may save someone a lifetime of misery—yourself!

If not, the Law of Return and karma will make sure you get the opportunity to "live your life over again," this time from the opposite point of view.

You may think this whole concept is completely wrong, can't be proven scientifically, or another million reasons why you prefer not to believe it. But what if my Spooks are right?

## *Cleaning Up After Charlatans*

Sometimes, I find myself picking up the pieces for some frightened, unhappy person who has just had a reading from another psychic or would-be psychic who just scared the hell out of them. This is probably the only time I get really angry anymore. I know the "psychic" will have to pay for the error by the Law of Return or karma, just as I would if I misuse or abuse the ability I have. The thing I find upsetting is that people spend years in fear and doubt because of something they were told by some long-ago fortune teller.

An aside: my Spooks are positive readers, and I'm only able to see negatives if there is a possibility of preventing a problem, or a need to prepare for a situation that can alter the final outcome. I believe that most honest psychics have similar principles, so if you hear something negative from a psychic, make sure it jibes with your own intuition before you get all bent out of shape.

I recently read for a couple and the young woman didn't really believe in the reading, especially when I told her that her father would die very soon. I seldom ever see death, so it was unusual and I had difficulty in presenting the information to her. She replied that it wouldn't matter to her. He'd deserted the family years before, was a real SOB, and meant nothing to her. She hadn't seen him and didn't care to.

Three weeks later, I got a call from this same young woman. She was in another state trying to put all of the pieces together so she could settle her father's estate. He had died very unexpectedly and she was the oldest child, so she was declared the executrix. He had land and he had money. It turned out even if there was no love or emotion, there was a financial and business arrangement that still needed to be settled. She took care of the details and received a nice sum of money for her trouble. He obviously owed her.

Another example: During one reading for a couple many years ago, a very strong impression came of danger in an automobile the next day. The Spooks wanted them to be extremely careful in driving on mountain roads, particularly one sharp curve. Then they went on to describe the surrounding. The couple called the next night to verify that when the exact setting came into view on the trip that day, they both remembered the warning and slowed down to a near stop, just before a tire blew out. They felt the advance warning may have saved their lives and I was just as surprised as they were by the accuracy of the description.

Sadly, some so-called psychics are far too free with messages of doom. Once, we were disturbed after midnight by a young woman knocking on the back door who had just had a reading from a psychic who told her she would commit suicide soon. Linda was told she had committed suicide at the age of twenty-nine in three previous lives and would repeat the pattern this time. Since she was twenty-nine years old at the time and going through a very difficult, depressing period in her life, nothing could have been a more dangerous or stupid prediction. We spent the next two hours reassuring Linda, found out that she had been contemplating suicide, which the psychic may have picked up, but convinced her that free will and her long-term goals in this life were the determining factor.

I read her palm, explaining the meaning and location of each significant line in her hand, showing her my hand, before letting her find the corresponding lines in her own hand. By this means Linda was able to find her marriage, but not until around thirty-five years of age, and the two children she would have. She had to locate her future in her own palm because it was there, not because I found a line and then gave an interpretation. Linda was also able to find the mark in her palm that indicated her current depressions, but also the box of protection around it, and the continuing life line beyond.

We also explained that no one can determine when another soul will die. That is between God and each individual soul. Before Linda left, she was able to laugh at her own fears and gullibility in listening to and believing a total stranger's dire predictions. That was thirty years ago, and Linda is happily married with two children, a son and daughter, just as the lines in her palm indicated.

Linda had a master's degree and state licenses, and she worked as a marriage, family, and child counselor for a large counseling center in a large city. She was extremely intelligent and capable but had been caught in a low point in her life. She might have ended it that night without the Spooks' intervention. They knew what to say and how to present it so she did her own reading, one that she could feel comfortable with.

This was one of the most serious and dangerous predictions I have personally ever encountered from another "reader," and I can't understand why anyone would place such fear on another soul. Had Linda not been wise enough to seek help from us or another source, that insane prediction could have become a self-fulfilling prophecy!

This is one reason I try to explain to all of the people for whom I read, that even though my Spooks may be very accurate, I can misinterpret the message. I also tell all of them not to design their lives around anything predicted in any reading ever, including mine. Even the "best" readers on their best days will be only 80 percent accurate. That leftover 20 percent allows for a lot of error, so plan your life with common sense and a good sprinkling of logic. It's a comfort to know that the future will be brighter, but also to remember that, "God helps those who help themselves."

## Beware of Roadside Psychics

The first reading I ever had as an adult from an outside source was really enlightening. I'd seen this gypsy palmistry sign on the highway for years and finally got enough courage to go for a reading with my sister. The room was filled with religious statues, trinkets, and brightly colored scarves and wall hangings. A crystal ball stood on the table. A middle-aged woman who looked like a character from a gypsy fortune teller B movie, complete with dangling earrings, was sitting in a wicker chair.

It seemed her goal in life was to convince me that a dark-haired woman had cast an evil spell on me and my entire family. When I tried to explain my beliefs in reincarnation and the goal of each individual soul, she didn't seem to hear me. She just kept adding more detail to the evil curse routine. Finally, I told her I didn't believe it, but even if this was true, what was the purpose? Oh boy! She could lift the spell by special powers. All I had to do was bring her a spool of blue thread, a leaf from a tree in my yard, and one of my husband's handkerchiefs and she would lift the spell. Oh yes, I also had to bring $50.

I couldn't believe what I was hearing. It was so totally irrational. I wondered if this was the same routine she gave all of her clients. How many fell for it? Her sign had been on the highway for a good many years, and it wasn't in need of paint.

Some years later, when I again found a psychic, it was an entirely different experience. She guided and helped our family through a number of rough spots, and she predicted most of the significant events in our lives. Even if she hadn't been a good, accurate reader, she was a very good "seat of the pants" therapist and counselor. I referred many people to her over the years and never had cause to doubt her. She later became one of my teachers and, as she put it, "Didn't teach [me] to read, just reawakened the psychic abilities [I]had brought into this life."

When I started to tell her about my previous experience with the gypsy fortune teller, she interrupted and gave me the whole spiel the gypsy had used with the following variance. "Madame S. told you to bring her a spool of blue thread, a leaf, $50, and a pair of your husband's dirty shorts! I don't know why she always asks for blue thread. Maybe she's sewing a blue circus tent!"

That was in 1970 and here we are thirty-five years later and I'm still hearing the same story from the people I read for. One wanted my client to bring her own underpants and $1,500, and another one in Bermuda wanted $2,000. I guess the price of lifting these terrible spells has gone up just like everything else.

Please don't fall for this con. It is taught to young gypsy women as one of the fear tactics used to scare clients into spending money. The only curse involved is the con being used by those psychics.

## Question Your Own Motives, Too

Speaking of manipulation, I have one woman who calls me from the East Coast who really tickles me. She is capable of asking the same question, one hundred different ways, in an attempt to get the answer she wants to hear. She also calls every new psychic she hears about, trying to find one that will play the game with her. I've called her on it and she laughs and admits it, but keeps right on trying.

My Spooks just won't let me provide the message people want to hear at the expense of the truth. The message doesn't change just because you may not like the predicted outcome. Since this client is usually involved with married men, you don't even have to be psychic to predict the typical end to most of her affairs. She wants every one to be "the one" and keeps trying to force a one-night-stand into a long-term relationship.

What I usually find in such cases is what the Spooks and I call the "sandbox syndrome." Typically, an educated, capable, intelligent woman is determined to force the current romance into becoming the lifelong, enduring relationship she is so desperately seeking. Usually the guy is just not interested in a long-term relationship, or any relationship, at this point in his life and just wants out. The woman feels rejected and inadequate, and blames herself for the whole problem instead of just letting go.

The Spooks suggest to her that she consider the possibility that she is a much older, more mature soul who chooses to get involved with younger souls who have not gone through the same number or types of experiences on the physical plane. She could consider her soul as having a master's degree and the men she insists on being involved with as being in kindergarten, thus creating the sandbox syndrome. I've explained that these younger souls are usually very attractive, lots of fun, have nice toys in the sandbox, but are not able to accept the relationship as more than just "playing."

When you take this theory one step further, it brings up the notion of getting sexually involved with children. Very few people ever want to even think about such behavior and it certainly gives them something to ponder.

The same is true with men who get involved with women who are so immature in the soul world that they only want to play house in the physical world. This leads to unhappy relationships and heartbreak. My advice? Try to find the soul who is actually looking for the same future and goals as you are. This has nothing to do with sex and physical attraction. While both of these things are important and necessary, they can really be distractions in the long-term advancement of your soul. You should want someone you like and enjoy the company of, and someone with whom you share the same lifetime goals.

I tell people that after fifty-four years of marriage, I still like my husband. He is my best friend and confidant. Years before, my sister was getting a divorce and said of her husband, "I love him. I just don't like him." At the time that seemed weird, but over the years and in readings for others this is the one remark that comes up most often. You can be in love with another soul, sexually and physically attracted, but you don't like the way that person treats others or behaves in serious situations. It is a difficult truth to face. If you don't like the person, you can't continue the game.

## *The Best Purpose for a Reading*

Through my Spooks, I try to help individual people make it through the day. I don't deal in world-shattering predictions, politics, and I don't want to be involved in criminal investigations. I have little patience with those who use their abilities to manipulate or control the lives of other people, or those who deliberately leave others in fear after a reading. If I'm not able to help individuals to deal with the situations in their lives, leave them with some help and a positive direction, then I'll quit doing readings. My Spooks have always pointed me toward a positive, helpful response when doing readings.

This is a good blueprint for what you should want out of a reading, then: insight, inspiration, and hope.

---

### PSYCHIC TIP: FIND THE RIGHT PSYCHIC

The choice is yours in finding a psychic. Be open to the process and be honest. Don't expect someone to tell you that you will be rich, beautiful, and famous, guaranteed. If it's too good to be true, it probably isn't true. Once in a while I come up with something that sounds like a typical gypsy fortune teller: "You will meet a dark, handsome, rich man, and be married in two weeks." If there is no alternative way to say what the Spooks are giving me, I will admit that it sounds too pat to me too, but that is what I'm getting. My own sister-in-law told me that she really hadn't believed it when the Spooks told me who she would meet and marry after my brother died. Her exact statement was, "I thought she was full of s---, until it happened" exactly as predicted.

Some people are convinced they were George Washington or Cleopatra in a past life because some other psychic gave them that impression. Funny, people never want to know if they were Jack the Ripper. Who you were means nothing. It's what you learned and what you did that matters. If everyone who wanted to be a specific famous person actually had lived in that person's era, the world would have been very crowded!

Come to either a reading or a healer with an open mind, then, to receive the best care and the most accurate information.

Try to find a reader or healer who is recommended by another person you respect who has been to see them. You often check with friends for the name of an attorney, doctor, and counselor or other professional when you need help. You'd be surprised at how many of those professionals also call me, so don't be afraid to ask around. If you just pick someone out of the telephone directory it will be the "luck of the draw." I usually only do readings for people who are being referred by one of my current clients. There is one small town in the Midwest where I have probably read for more than half of the citizens, but most people don't even know it, unless they talk to each other.

You will benefit from the psychic help, either in a reading or through alternative medicine, and probably get some answers that have been troubling you all of your life. Not long ago, I was amazed and pleased to find out the Spooks gave security and direction to a twelve-year-old boy who was convinced he was going to die when he was fourteen, so "why bother?" The Spooks were able to help him realize that this was a soul memory from a previous life, but not part of the plan he had made for his current life. Now he is busy making plans for college, football, and a career in sports medicine—all of the things he really wanted to do, but thought he would not be able to accomplish. He has a busy life planned and great goals! And, he will succeed. His mother and grandfather both say his attitude has changed so much, it is like having a new person in the house!

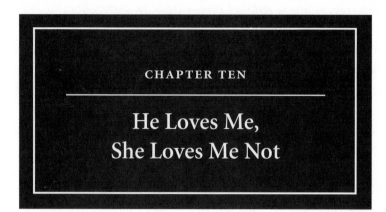

# CHAPTER TEN

# He Loves Me,
# She Loves Me Not

One of the most important and difficult tasks we face on this earth is our search for love and a soul to share our lives with. It is an ongoing search our entire lives, and we are sometimes "searching for love in all the wrong places" or not recognizing the real emotion even when we find it. One very cynical soul I knew felt love was just a very addictive form of self-hypnosis created just to get us into our karma.

On the astral plane or soul world, a blending of two souls—in what we would consider just a hug—is so complete and intimate that we try to find or replace that during our physical life on earth. Very close to this "soul" hug is the great love you feel toward your family, friends, and pets. Yet we still want more, and the closest thing we have to that feeling and pleasure involves sex on the earth.

## *Sex ≠ Love*

We confuse the issue when the other gender is involved. For this reason we get sex confused with love and try to separate the two. You really can't. To be complete, they have to go together. Your own experiences have proven to you that sex without love can be an empty and tawdry experience that leaves you feeling empty and used. When you really love the other soul, you don't ever want to lose that person or the experience. So we continue the search and become very disappointed when something happens to the perfect union or relationship we think we have found.

At times this can be a very one-sided affair, and the person you consider your perfect soul mate may have other situations they have to clear before you can get together. One lady I read for had been engaged at eighteen years of age to the perfect man. They had bought a house, had the wedding all planned and something happened. Neither of them could even remember the reason for the argument, but it was enough to call off the wedding. Years later they met again. Both had been married and both were now widowed—their respective spouses had died at approximately the same time. She had two sons and he had not been able to have children, due to some physical reason which at that point didn't matter. They started seeing each other and were married within six months. Now they had the two sons they wouldn't have had and the grandchildren to share and enjoy in the future.

They were extremely happy and never could understand why they had split up when they were just kids. It really didn't matter. It was just supposed to happen. According to the Spooks, she had promised to allow those two souls to come through her as sons and that opportunity would have been lost had she married at eighteen. Yes, they could have adopted, but all of the details so important to their lives would have changed.

Sometimes souls find each other when they are much too young. I'm not sure why; maybe just to verify that the future mate is here and it will be all right a few years down the road. One particular instance was my oldest son and his future wife being in the same first grade class. (I ask you, what are the odds of that happening?) Obviously six is much too young to meet but they did, then promptly forgot each other until they were in college. The Spooks had predicted their meeting at the age of twenty-one, right down to the fact that he would be giving a birthday party he didn't want to give for a friend and she would be talked into going to the party by another friend, when she really didn't want to go. Oh well, it was preplanned and arranged in the soul world. They have now been married for over thirty years.

Only each of us knows how or why we set up the intricate details of meeting our soul mate, something that was done before we were born.

## *Careful Around Those Triggers!*

Prior to our birth, we arrange details, including certain phrases, situations, or a look that will be remembered by our soul when we return to earth. This is the trigger point that gets your attention and sets the future bond in motion. I know that one phrase used by my husband certainly got my attention. I have never forgotten it to this day.

When we met, I was working at the Service Club on a U.S. Army Base and he had just returned home from the front lines in Korea. My brother had been injured very badly in Korea and I moved in with my sister-in-law to be a companion and protector (ha). We planned to be near my brother, who was in the hospital undergoing multiple surgeries. Needless to say, I thought I was the belle of the ball as one of only six single women on an army base. It took something special to get or hold my attention.

One of the other GIs was trying to set up a double date with me. The plan was that I was to get a date with one of my friends for Rockie, and the other GI would be my date. I wasn't too keen on this and got the other GI to suggest that Rockie be my date. To this suggestion Rockie responded, "Her? I wouldn't take her to a dog fight!"

When I got over being mad, I decided to get even. Three months later, the other GI was part of our honor guard at the military wedding on the base.

The phrase was the one key that got my attention and which I never forgot. All Rockie says is, "Well, I never did take you to a dog fight!" Rockie says he knew all the time he was in the front lines in Korea that he would be OK because he was coming home to marry a blond girl with blue eyes and have a blond-haired, blue-eyed son, so I guess the look is what got his attention.

We both knew we would marry after the first date and told our relatives that. After that, we were both firmly convinced we knew each other from somewhere but just couldn't place where or when. It was something about the eyes and obviously a soul memory. We just knew each other.

## *Watch the Eyes*

They say eyes are the "windows of the soul." I believe this is true, especially considering some of the stories I've been told in readings. Many people have mentioned the eyes of the person they love or are involved with as being so beautiful, deep, special, that I know this is a universal experience. This is one of the ways we know and remember another soul.

Many years ago I was telephoned by a lady I'll call Carolyn. She was in tears and had difficulty explaining why she was calling and what had happened. It was March and her husband had just died in December. He was her second husband—his death was sudden and unexpected as they had been married only five months—and he had no physical problems. She adored him, and so did her two sons from her first marriage.

The Spooks reassured her that her husband did not consciously expect to die at that time either. He had simply forgotten his previous commitment, as we all do, to leave at that age. If he had consciously remembered that he would die in just five months, he would not have let himself fall in love and marry. There was a purpose in the entire set of circumstances that neither could understand, but it would become clear in time.

He was still watching over her and would arrange for her to meet another wonderful guy to take his place. The Spooks then told her, through me, several of her husband's mannerisms, about his beautiful blue eyes with the lashes that were ridiculously long for a man, and that the new love would resemble him in several distinct ways. He would come into her life in November and she would remarry in May. This was March and there is no way she would believe one bit of this. I laughed and told her that she would send me a wedding invitation.

I got a call in November. The man had come into her life just as predicted and his story was just too good to be true. He was the chief of police in the little town where she lived. He had been deserted by his first wife when he was just a young man. She had run off with another man and left him with her two children, whom he adopted. He had raised the children alone and they were both graduating from college that year. He promised Carolyn that if they married he would see to it that her sons were given every opportunity he had guaranteed to his two adopted children. He even looked and acted like her deceased husband.

"Oh yes," she added when we talked. "The eyes. He has my husband's eyes." They were married the following May, as predicted, and I was sent a wedding invitation.

I've talked to her since and he kept the promise he made. Her sons are now both in college with plans for real careers. The family has been very happy and she can only bless her deceased husband for the help he has given all of them. No jealousy, no guilt, just love and happiness. Jealousy does not exist on the astral or soul plane and her deceased husband was very pleased with his part in making the dream come true, even if he was no longer physically involved. Her deceased husband remained in the group as one of the guides and the entire group continued to advance. This was all part of the elaborate arrangement so these three souls could complete a karmic cycle and the entire situation was carefully planned before any of them were born. They planned it.

## Eyes Across the Room

Another wedding invitation story was just finalized last fall. I had been reading for Donna for many years, during which time she was involved with Doug. He was a workaholic, but so was she, and they didn't get to spend much time together unless they took a trip. They made a point of vacationing together and had some very memorable times.

They owned property together in another state, but they just didn't seem to have time to create the permanent relationship she really wanted. They were both just too busy with their own businesses, children, finances, etc.

In a reading, the Spooks told her she was about to meet another man at a party. It would be a meeting of the eyes "across a crowded room" situation, but they would both feel it. The Spooks also gave her his initials, something they rarely do. (If they do, I don't repeat the letters even if I hear them. I had learned years ago that if you gave a person a first name or an initial they would try to force every person they met with that name or initial into the love frame they are busy creating.) She says I gave her his first name, but I don't remember doing it.

They took it slow and allowed the relationship to develop naturally over the next two years. They found they had so many things in common. They both loved to play golf and were very good, nearly at the level of professional golfers. For this reason they were able to enjoy a game together or when teamed together in tournaments.

They were married last October and I received an invitation to that wedding also. I never go to any of the weddings. I just collect the announcements as remembrances for the Spooks. We have accumulated quite a collection over the years.

## *In Love, Don't Force the Issue*

People are always calling me and saying they "need to fix" a situation. "I need to make him love me again . . . how can I . . . why won't he . . ." These and other similar statements boil down to: How can I make it happen?

It is almost impossible for a soul to force something into happening, regardless of the obstacles the Spooks set up. It is just about as difficult to keep ourselves from trying to make it happen! Probably the biggest mistake we make in the physical world is to "try to make things happen." We still try to force it, even when everything is going wrong! We are firmly convinced we can fix it or force something to adapt to our desires. All we need is a little cooperation or maybe a magic spell or something.

This just is not possible. You can't make someone love you. Either the feeling, chemistry, or attraction is there, or it is not. The feeling has to be two sided and mutual. Perhaps the soul you are trying so hard to attract has a different goal in this lifetime and it doesn't include you.

When I mention forcing a relationship or holding on after it's really over, it brings to mind thousands of individuals who have called with the typical heartbreak story. One in particular was so determined to get the love of her life back that she was even driving by his home at all hours of the day and night to see who he was with, what he was doing, etc. She was basically stalking him. Every time she called it was with another scheme to get his attention. It got to the point she didn't care if it was positive or negative attention—she just wanted him to acknowledge that she was still there.

She still had some of his belongings in her possession and decided to use them to get him to notice her. One of her last plans involved his hunting rifle and various means of returning it. The Spooks strongly recommended that she give the gun either to the local police department to return to him or to her brother, but get it out of her possession. She needed to face the fact that it was over and get on with her own life before she ended up in jail over some stupid mistake or misunderstanding regarding his possessions. They also recommended therapy with a professional counselor.

I have another client who has some of her previous boyfriend's books and is constantly trying to think of a clever way to return them. Not quite as dangerous as a gun, but still as foolish. I've told her that he doesn't care about the books and doesn't even remember loaning them to her. They are just paperbacks anyway, not expensive collectors' editions and she could always mail them to him. Once again, she is trying to make something happen and it just won't work because you can't make someone love you or stay with you unless the love was prearranged on the other side.

Let go, get on with your life so you can be available to meet the person who is just around the corner. He or she may be the one you've really been waiting for. The other possibility is that you aren't ready to meet that special soul yet either. Maybe there are other things you need to accomplish first.

## *Sometimes, Let Her Go*

I once read for a young man whose wife had just told him she wanted a divorce. Her only explanation was that he was not a good husband, didn't support the family adequately, didn't take her out to fancy restaurants and on trips. (They had just returned from a week in Hawaii.) He was already working two jobs and left the home feeling like a total failure. His sister talked him into calling me. The Spooks said he would have the answer to the cause and reason for the divorce, but wouldn't know for two months. He would want the divorce and not to worry, as he would meet his future wife at work.

He didn't believe or understand any of this until he found out that his wife of fifteen years had been involved in an affair with the next door neighbor for two years while she was belittling and berating him, insisting he work more and more hours to buy her the things she just had to have. He met his current wife at work as predicted, and they have had one of the most loving and caring marriages for the past twenty-five years.

During the years, I've also gotten to know his current wife and she could never believe any woman would be foolish enough to let him get away. His ex-wife is now working on her fourth marriage. Maybe she had a lot of previous debts to clear, but she may be making more in the process. I guess only she and her guides know the answer to that.

## *Judge Not . . .*

This reminds me of the interesting client who was getting her fifth divorce and called, firmly convinced she was a total loser, did everything wrong, and would never have a real love or relationship. This crying tirade included some self-destructive comments. The Spooks forced her to read her own palm to help her understand what was really happening.

I told her she had seven marriage lines in her hand and to quit the self-destructive plans. She was doing just what she had planned to do during this lifetime. She had been born with seven lines in her hand and even she had to admit you couldn't try to convince anyone that a baby was a promiscuous woman or a loser. This just meant she had seven souls she owed or seven souls who owed her a debt this lifetime. She was taking care of seven karmic debts all in one life. This was a big responsibility. I told her where the lines were in her hand and she located all seven just as predicted.

We then discussed how these lines indicated emotional attachments, loves, or marriages. Then the Spooks told her she had finished with five of the karmic debts and only had two to go. She realized she could actually be proud of what she had accomplished already when she looked at it from a karmic point of view. The Spooks also told her to look toward the future. Her next relationship would be a very good one and last for more than twenty-five years. She responded with a "How did you know?" I didn't, but the Spooks did. Oddly enough, this had always been a secret goal of hers, to have a twenty-fifth wedding anniversary.

I'm also reminded of the lady who was married, had twin girls, and got a divorce. She remarried and had two boys, then got divorced. By this time, the twin girls were grown up and on their own, but for some reason she and her first husband got back together and were remarried. This put the first husband in the position of raising the other man's sons. The same man who had raised his daughters. Karma? You bet. I'd sure like to be allowed to go back into that lifetime to see what caused the situation to start in the first place. When the boys were raised, the couple again chose to divorce. She is now working on her fifth marriage. A lot of karma and debts are being cleared in this situation by all the souls involved.

Occasionally I will help a client find lines in their palms when it is important for them to realize they will have children and will marry. It may not be this week and maybe not this year, but this is part of the long-term plan their soul made before being born.

## Maybe You're Not Destined for Love

Some souls make the deliberate choice to not marry or create a long-term relationship during a particular lifetime. Look at the individuals who become priests, monks, and nuns. This is their choice, yet even they sometimes find someone for whom they are willing to break their vows.

Some individuals get caught up in the game when they see all of their friends involved, and when various relatives keep asking, "When are you going to get married and settle down?" or "I want grandbabies."

Be sure you are looking for a need of your own and not one implanted in your mind by others around you. Some people lead long, happy, and productive lives without a spouse or permanent relationship. I've read for some individuals who are perfectly happy to be alone. They just want to know how to stop the pushing and interference in their lives from family members and friends.

My brother's wife chose not to remarry after he died when they were both only twenty-eight years old. Once I asked her why she had not re-married. (See, good old family members, trying to fix her up!) We certainly would have understood and been happy for her. We were very close and the four of us had lived together on several occasions. She explained that in fourteen years as a widow she had never met anyone she wanted to have across the breakfast table from her every morning. She was perfectly happy to live alone, which she did until her death from a massive heart attack at the age of forty-two. This was her choice. I'm sure they are back together now and are part of the family core on the other side or busy doing their own thing. Remember, their choice!

## *Find Love on the Internet? Fat Chance*

Since the advent of the Internet, many individuals have tried using this means of meeting prospective mates. It really sounds like a great way to get to know someone, kind of like writing letters until you feel comfortable with the soul on the other end—like the pen pals from long ago. You don't have to go to singles clubs or bars and it really seems ideal, unless in walks the Internet Gigolo.

Often, I talk to women who are communicating with Mr. Wonderful on the Internet and are firmly convinced he will be the love of their lives. They have not met the individual yet, but he is writing all of the right things and they just know he will be perfect because their Internet communication is so open, honest, etc. etc. A few days or weeks later I get the "heartbreak hotel" call when they discover their god has feet of clay that are firmly planted in a marriage with a wife, children, bills, boredom, and all of the rest. He is sitting in the bedroom at the computer, in his own fantasy world, while his wife and children are in the living room.

One of my clients really got pulled into one of these long-distance romances. He sounded just perfect, they had the same interests, and he was well-read and exciting, single, and an executive in a large corporation.

He continued the communication with all the frills until they were supposed to meet. His plan was to fly into her city and spend the weekend. This was scheduled several times, but he always cancelled at the last minute due to some serious business circumstance beyond his control that prevented him from making the trip. After this had happened about four times she decided to surprise him and flew to his city to meet him. She just knew he would be thrilled and she would be the big happy surprise. She got the big surprise. It turned out he was married, with five children, and apparently had been playing the Internet game for quite a while.

As all of the details were revealed and the weekend progressed she learned more about his ongoing infidelity. This was not the first time his wife had caught him in one of these games, but she chose to stay married for the security needed to raise five children. My client met the wife and decided to show her how to check up on him on the Internet to see who he was lying to and communicating with. It would make it easier to catch him in the future. Another surprise for my client was that he had several other girlfriends besides her that she discovered in his Internet files. He was a very busy boy.

According to the wife, he spent every night on the Internet chat room in the bedroom and didn't want her or the children to interrupt him. Doesn't that sound like a real great guy to meet? He lived in a total fantasy world and could be anyone he wanted to be on the Internet. The whole purpose was to bolster his middle-aged ego—no love, no caring, no interest other than to con some unsuspecting woman who was sincerely looking for love, obviously in all the wrong places.

The other Internet love story, which I was told by the woman who experienced it, was even more outrageous. This client lived back East and had been communicating with her Mr. Right in Australia for over six months. She was so totally infatuated with her perfect Australian love that she was in the midst of quitting her job, selling her home and all of her belongings to move to be with him in Australia when the e-mail suddenly stopped. She tried everything to reach him and finally got an e-mail about a month later. The e-mail said her love had died suddenly from a heart attack and the person who was writing her was his son. He had found her name and number on his father's computer when he was settling the estate. He felt notifying her was the only decent thing to do and grieved with her over the loss of his father.

She was heartbroken. Then she decided she wanted to send an appropriate memorial for her love to be placed on his gravesite. You can only imagine her shock and anger to find there was no gravesite. He had not died. He had just pretended to be dead and wrote the e-mails as his own son to get rid of her and stop the whole game. He had apparently decided it had gone too far and he didn't want her showing up in Australia since this would be difficult to explain to his wife!

One of the other Internet tales I've been told is really pretty funny. My client agreed to meet Mr. Wonderful at the bar in a large hotel downtown before they went out to dinner. She gave him a description of herself, including the red hair, green eyes, size eight, etc. He told her he was tall and very attractive to which she responded, "Looks aren't everything. The personality is what really matters." This scared him and he asked her what that meant. He asked, "Are you really ugly?" Pretty blunt!

Then she met him. The Spooks, it seemed, were testing her attitude about looks not mattering. She could only describe him as a living, breathing Ichabod Crane's brother, tall, scraggly, hook nosed, and awkward. She knew it had to be him the moment she walked into the bar and saw the least attractive man in town standing there, ogling her like a box of candy.

This was not even the worst part of the date. He read prices off of the menu to her and insisted that she only have a dinner salad, which was all he ordered. He apparently knew the date was not going anywhere from the look on her face and didn't want to waste money if there would be no payoff. She described him as rude, crude, and unattractive. She didn't try any more Internet dates after that one. She is happily married now and has a daughter, but she didn't meet her husband on the Internet.

Another lady I read for met a man on the Internet and agreed to meet him in another city, not hers and not his. This is a really dangerous thing to do. He obviously had something to hide but he might have been some kind of pervert or murderer. No one would have known who she met or why she went to that city if something had happened.

Please keep in mind that on the Internet you have to accept everything you are told at face value and there is little opportunity to check on the details, like wives, children, other girlfriends, or competition. You assume people are being as honest with you as you are being with them. The problem is that some people treat this as an entertaining hobby and don't feel any guilt over the lies they are telling. They just assume you are lying too and it's just a game. A very painful, sick game.

If you do want to play the game there are several things you can do to protect yourself:

- Do arrange a meeting in person as soon as possible, with others present.
- Meet in your own hometown and let others know your plan.
- Ask for a phone number, day and night, and call. If there is a wife, husband, or live in they won't want to give you their number, or will give you a false one. Do not accept only a work number. You want to know their living arrangement.
- Don't get too intimate or give too many details to this person.
- Remember that the picture may actually be of a best friend.
- Do use common sense. The Internet is not just a sexual playground. Finally, don't be so gullible and willing to believe or forgive anything.

I've been told some people actually do meet their future mates on the Internet, but I've never read for anyone who had a pleasant or happy experience. It seems like it would be such a good tool for people to communicate and get to know one another, but someone always wants to improve their own image, forgetting they will eventually meet and have to try to explain. Maybe they think that if they are able to make a good enough impression, the other partner will forgive the little exaggerations, but a wife and children are not little exaggerations.

## *Fear Will Handcuff You*

Another lady I read for is well educated, works on the parole board for the prison systems and felt she really understood human nature. Even with all of these pluses, she stayed in an angry, frustrating marriage for twenty years. Why? Fear, uncertainty about the future, and sometimes just the feeling that there may never be anyone else in her life. This is the syndrome that keeps someone tied into a mess with the thought that "he or she is better than nothing." Sometimes it is really difficult to end a relationship even when you know you just need to pull the plug. When I first heard from her, she was fed up and wanted to file for divorce but her husband had told her he would kill her or himself if she ever tried. He was verbally abusive, but had never tried physical abuse, was a habitual gambler, stayed unemployed as much as possible, and basically just sponged off of her. The Spooks told her to stand up to him, throw him out, and file.

The next time he started the verbal abuse and threats, she called the police and had him removed. It was so much easier to actually do than she had thought. The divorce was long and ugly, and he even tried to collect spousal support since she had been supporting him for the past fifteen years, even paying all of his gambling debts. Then, to add insult to injury, she was forced by a court order to continue his medical insurance for three years. She was furious at him, than saw the humor in it. She received every receipt for anything the medical insurance paid and the real kick was seeing just how often he was getting his Viagra refilled! They'd had many disagreements over his inability to function sexually, and he had always blamed her. Now she knew better and had the evidence to back her.

She met another man and within a year they were living together, and planning a wedding. There was a lot of opposition from his family, particularly his mother, but they were going ahead. He died suddenly of a heart attack, but the Spooks say he was only there to help her for a short time. A permanent relationship would have been extremely difficult with his mother's interference. She knew this, but still felt she wanted to try. We know someone else is already on the way and this time she believes it. I expect to hear from her any day that her real love is finally with her.

The great part is that she will never fear changing her life if the situation isn't right. She also believes she will not be alone—but believes sometimes being alone is better than staying with someone you can't stand. That's a big change from her original fear that kept her in a twenty-year-long losing marriage.

In the past, people stayed in very unhappy marriages "for the sake of the children," even after the children were grown and gone. They were often in love/hate relationships. They loved to hate each other, and hated to love each other, but were still bragging about a fiftieth wedding anniversary. Often individuals stayed in very unhappy relationships just because they didn't want to split their assets and have to share the net worth with an ex-partner. Some still do. I feel sorry for them because they place material things above happiness and the growth of their soul, completely forgetting that the material and financial things are just of this world. You really can't take it with you, but you can create the karma to be forced to return and lose everything you accumulate, over and over, until you gain the proper perspective. You will choose this path because your soul knows what is really important and wants to continue progressing. Now some people actually celebrate the divorce anniversary as a special date to remember.

One lady I read for has been in an on-again, off-again affair with a married man who is over sixty-five. She is near fifty-five, and this has been going on for the past ten years. He has a large farm, money, and a big family. They have just been waiting for his wife to die so he won't have to go through a divorce and property settlement because these belongings are so important to him. Can you imagine wasting ten years of your life waiting for another soul to die? The funniest part is that the wife will probably outlive both of them and get to keep it all.

There is no guarantee how long you will be with a new love. It may be just a very exciting and interesting weekend or it may be a lifetime. It all depends on what your soul was supposed to learn or experience with the other soul. The problems only arise when you try to make a long-term relationship out of a long weekend. Don't try to make things happen, but be willing to go a little out of your way or walk away with peace and understanding. Look for the lesson just learned.

## *Know When to Fold Your Hand*

Knowing when to let go and allow both souls to continue to grow and experience new loves and lives is difficult. Each soul has to come to that decision on its own. Sometimes the Spooks can give them the reassurance they need to let go and start over. Most individuals who make the decision are very happy to have their freedom of choice back and call to say so. Others want the Spooks to guarantee a new love and find the soul for them. We can't do this.

One lady I've read for went through the ugliest divorce of all time, managed to keep custody of the children, knew she would never forgive the SOB she had just divorced, and would never be able to even be in the same room. She just remarried in a beautiful ceremony at Lake Tahoe where all of her children, her new stepchildren, and her nieces and nephews each gave the bride one long-stemmed red rose at the wedding to create the bride's bouquet of eleven roses. The following week, her ex-husband showed up at her door with a bottle of champagne, a card of congratulations, and tears in his eyes. He had just heard she was remarried and he finally realized what he had thrown away. Too little and too late!

She still thinks he is an SOB, but can hold a civil conversation with him that involves the children. Hopefully, by the time there are grandchildren, the anger and frustration will be just a dim memory. I've seen some former mates dance together at their children's weddings, so anything is possible. Time really does heal all wounds.

On a couple of occasions, the Spooks have recommended that people raise their heads and start looking around at other individuals in the area. Guys or gals are flirting with them and trying to attract their attention every day, and they are ignoring all the signals. Make eye contact (remember the eyes?) with individuals that you find attractive, particularly when you find them looking at you. Just a little smile or a wink may be all that is necessary to give them the confidence to approach you. Remember ladies, guys get rejected a lot when they are trying to find a new love. Try to be a little more willing to give them the encouragement needed. Also remember that some don't need encouragement as much as they need a cold shower, so don't go overboard.

Be willing to be a little patient as you search. The soul you made all of the special arrangements to meet is still out there. Sometimes you or they just get caught up in a little detour.

---

**PSYCHIC TIP: HOW TO FIND THE LOVE OF YOUR LIFE**
Keep your head up and notice your surroundings. Your new love may be standing on his head across the street trying to get your attention!

Remember the Law of Return from the previous chapters. If you are a user, you will be used. If you are a giver, you will receive. If you keep having the same type of experiences, take an honest look at your behavior. What are you putting out that keeps coming back?

Allow love to happen; don't try to make it happen.

When it's over, let it go. You can't make someone love you and they can't make you love them. Love is a karmic feeling and it isn't always supposed to be forever—just until a lesson is taught or learned!

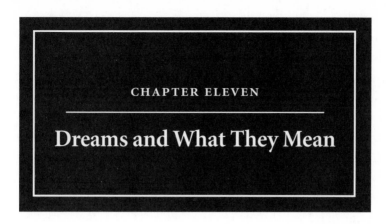

# CHAPTER ELEVEN

# Dreams and What They Mean

Most of us dream every night and often don't remember the dream at all—or only remember disjointed bits and pieces. In dream labs, researchers have been able to determine the time of a dream by eye movement and brain waves. However, what they can't do is tell you what the dream means. Sometimes you are the only one who really understands, and sometimes it is nearly impossible to distinguish between dreams and astral projections that you remember vividly.

Dreams come from a multitude of sources. They can be a rehash of something that is happening in your life with which you are having difficulty; the dream is your higher self or soul trying to give you clarification or make you see a possibility you have been overlooking during the day. We get so involved in just trying to make it through the day, we sometimes forget we can get help at night just by asking for it. Ask for an answer before you go to sleep. Just think of the problem you are facing and ask your Spooks to give you some help. Then put a pad and pencil beside the bed and write down what you remember when you awaken, even if it is at 2:00 AM. Don't try to wait until morning, because you will forget.

## *Some Dreams Are Postcards from the Astral Plane*

Some dreams are actually mixed experiences from the astral plane filtered through our physical brains. We don't really understand everything from the other side. Our physical brains aren't capable of it. Just try to put some of the symbols together and see if it gives you an answer to something much more important than the daily hustle and bustle.

Dreams or memories from your trip to the astral plane at night can be helpful to understanding why you are here and what you are working on. They can also help you realize you are not alone, especially when you have a particularly vivid dream about someone you love who has died. You usually awaken feeling more secure about where they are and that you will be with them again. Of course when my dad was dreaming about being with my brother, drinking whiskey, playing cards, and splitting up the territory, it made us think twice!

One of my clients had a dream just before Christmas that was probably an out-of-body experience. In the dream, she decided that she was probably already dead and, if so, she could fly. She decided to fly out to California and see what we were doing. She called me the next day and described the scene from her dream and guess what? She had actually dropped in on us. She saw me and my daughter helping wrap Christmas gifts for abused children. We were together in a large room with about ten other people, and we had children's gifts spread all over the floor to facilitate assembly-line gift wrapping. She described this scene perfectly. She decided to fly—and apparently she did.

## *Some Dreams Are Precognitive*

Some people have precognitive dreams, dreams that later come true. Others dream of impending disasters such as plane crashes or assassinations. Some people with this ability find it devastating. They know a disaster is going to occur and they have no control over it, can't prevent it, and no one believes them. Not a gift most people would want to have. Most of those I know with this ability try to stop the dreams, or just choose to ignore them.

Not long ago we were awakened at 2:30 AM by our twenty-four-year-old grandson who is in the U.S. Army and had recently returned from a year in Iraq. He called to say he was scared to death. He had just dreamed that our house had burned down and he wanted his dad (who lives in the second house on our property) to check the wiring in the morning. I promised him we would listen and take care of it. We bought new smoke alarms for both houses and checked what we could on the wiring. I don't know if the dream was precognition or just a warning, but we acted on it. The houses are old and the wiring is bad, so good sense requires us to pay attention. When a young man who received the Bronze Star in Iraq calls and says he is scared to death, you listen!

My mother had precognitive dreams all the time. They were very disturbing in their accuracy. This is one of her great-grandsons, and while I don't know if he inherited the ability or not, we won't take any chances. When he called back, I told him what we had done. If the houses burned now, hopefully we would be on the outside watching and that seemed to be OK with him.

## Most Dreams Represent the Working-Out of Problems

On another occasion I got a call from one of my regular clients, very upset about a dream that in her mind pointed toward her mother's impending death. In the dream, she and her father are standing in the kitchen, cutting up vegetables, with tears running down their faces. They are talking about her mom, and both are very sad. She thought this meant her mother would die soon and she and her father would be left alone afterward.

Rockie told her it was not her mother who was leaving. Working in the kitchen together with her father while discussing the mother just meant they were working on the same problem together that concerned the mother—not that the mother was dead and they were mourning.

Several months later, her father died, and she realized what the dream really meant was the amount of difficulty involved for all members of the family in caring for the mother. She could finally understand how difficult it had been for her father to care for his very demanding wife. This was probably why they were both crying in the dream. Incidentally, five years have gone by and she is still caring for the mother—who is still very demanding.

## Dreams of Lives Past

Some dreams are soul memories, actual memories of a past life, and these can be very strange indeed. Usually, if the dream involved seeing yourself and others around you wearing clothing from a different period, or being involved in something obviously from history, it is probably a soul memory.

One couple I read for together told Rockie and me their peculiar dream, one they had both experienced repeatedly during their lives. In the husband's dream, he is playing a game of croquet or something similar with mallets and balls in the backyard of a beautiful old colonial home next to a river. Suddenly, the tranquil scene is disturbed by something shaped like a saucer flying just over the top of the river. They all stop and stare until it goes out of sight. Airplanes don't exist and they are all upset and confused over what they just saw. Nothing known to mankind at that time can fly!

Her dream is the other side of his. She is flying just over the river watching the people in funny old clothes playing a game in the backyard. The people stop the game, shout and point at her and her friends in the aircraft. She describes everything about the house, just the same as he does.

Rockie told them it had too much detail just to be imagination. It is very possible that it actually happened for both of them in a previous life. Flying saucers have been seen for a long time. They are not just peculiar to us in our time.

The record of everything that has ever happened exists in the astral plane, and your previous experiences are also imprinted in your memory. Sometimes, something comes back to the surface. These two had been together in many lives and could remember at least this one experience. They are very young and may have additional memories that resurface as they get older—maybe in dreams or maybe in actual waking memories. I asked them to let us know.

## *Dreams Point the Way Toward Spiritual Growth*

Another of my female clients called, upset because her dream had been of men popping up out of the ground in an area of new building. Then, all of a sudden a man's dismembered leg flew up out of the ground. She kept running to get away and found herself on a beautiful green golf course. Rockie's interpretation was pretty easy. She was allowing men to pop into her life all of the time and this prevented her from reaching her own new house or who she wanted to become. The leg popping up showed her confusion about her direction. If she continued to move forward and not be constantly sidetracked, she would ultimately reach the serenity she sought, which was represented by the green grass and peacefulness. Green represents healing, which would indicate the healing of her soul. She was actually running from one relationship to another, on a frantic search for "Mr. Wonderful." When she quit jumping in and out of short-term relationships, her whole life turned around. She is married now, with two children and is very happy.

## *Dreams Recur for a Reason*

Children's recurrent dreams often have to do with the direction their souls will be taking and what they will be working on when they become adults. A dream that my husband Rockie had repeatedly as a child was to find himself floating gently down from the balcony of a theater, to land softly, open his right hand, and find a coin in it. Sometimes he would then see a beautiful, white stallion rear up on his hind legs and paw the air while beautiful, sparkling fountains poured out of its head.

When he grew up and started to interpret dreams, he understood that the gentle floating represented the dream state, the sparkling fountain on the stallion head represented knowledge, and white indicated purity. The stallion represented the strength and power of his gift. The coin? It was just one coin, small change, so would indicate little change for his soul. The right hand was significant because it represented the male side of his soul and giving, rather then taking. He would be continuing to work in the psychic field he already understood and continue to give to others during this lifetime.

Our daughter Debbi had a recurrent dream as a child in which she walked around, and by, rectangular pools of water, on very tiny paths of dirt. The paths were only about six inches wide, making it necessary to walk very carefully with one foot just in front of the other. She had to be careful not to lose her balance. When she grew up and reminded us of this recurring dream, it was easy to see the pools representing the spiritual side of the soul and the astral plane. The paths of dirt represented the physical plane, earth.

This dream seems to have been very prophetic, as she has been balancing the physical necessity of continuing on the earthly plane, walking the straight and narrow, and taking one day at a time with the spiritual. During her lifetime, the astral plane has always been present, either through automatic writing, healing, or teaching. Debbi has been involved in herbal and natural medications for a long time and for a while had her own store that sold herbs. She has a master's degree in nursing and is a nurse practitioner. At the same time, she is learning the Reiki healing method and crystal healing techniques. She doesn't see any conflict with doing all forms together. Quite a balancing act; most people would have difficulty with it. I think this is part of walking the narrow paths through and around the spiritual ponds.

The dream I remember as a child is very frightening. In it, I would be hiding, usually on the roof of my parent's home. There was a loud noise close by, similar to a heart beating, and a voice saying, "Blue-black blood." I would look down on the ground and discover a dark pool of blue-black blood and remain hiding.

Remember the chapter with colors? Well, Rockie and the Spooks were able to interpret this dream after I finally got the courage to discuss it. Blue represents truth and reality. Black represents curiosity and death. Blood symbolizes life. The dream was letting me know I would learn to work with other people to teach the truth about life and death. The fear I felt was the fear all of us feel when we start working with or discovering the unknown. The fear of death is something we are all born with. The strange sound similar to a beating heart represented the ability to listen and learn from the astral plane. There was really nothing to fear; it was just another direction message for my adult life, a message I hid from for a long time.

These examples show why dream interpretation is a highly personal matter and requires that you work to understand what dreams mean in your life.

## Your Emotions: The Beginning Point of Dream Interpretation

When starting to interpret a dream, Rockie always asks how the individual felt at the time of the dream. This can be very enlightening. What might appear to be a nightmare may be more of a prophecy—like one particular dream of mine. I dreamed that Rockie and I were standing on a bridge overlooking a very large deep pool. A huge fish—the size of a whale—was swimming back and forth. There was a small boy standing beside me. Suddenly, the fish leaped out of the water and grabbed the small boy with its mouth and pulled him into the pool. The fish bit the child in half and took one half back under the water with him. I tried to jump off the bridge to save the child. Rockie restrained me from jumping in, saying, "Stop, just watch and see what happens!" He had to keep shouting it, because I wasn't listening. At that moment, the fish jumped back up and disappeared with the rest of the child. When I awakened, I was furious because I couldn't save the child.

This dream occurred about twenty years ago. As Rockie gave me the interpretation, I realized it wasn't a nightmare, but a vivid prophecy of the future. The fish represents Christ, religion, and faith; the water represents the spiritual side of life and the astral plane. A small child is the same symbol in my cards for "psychic, dreams, new ideas, child." The meanings are the same for the dream world. As Rockie explained it, the dream just showed that I would be learning more about the psychic field in my dreams and through new ideas coming in two gulps, or stages. This was shown by the fish taking the first gulp, then being hidden for a while, before he returned for the rest of the child—ideas, or psychic information.

This has proved to be even more accurate than I realized at the time. I am currently just completing the second phase. While Rockie was ill I did not do readings for nearly six years. I just returned to do readings and psychic work a couple of years ago. When I sent letters to my old clients, the response was unbelievable. They had been *waiting* for me and my Spooks to start reading again. My Spooks are better and more accurate than ever. The second gulp is now—and not at all what it seemed in the dream.

In my dreams, Rockie is always the strongest soul, telling me to wait, or just picking up the pieces for me. Another dream I had illustrates this. He and I are on air mattresses going down a very swift and dangerous stream, past rocks and rapids. In the dream, I am finding the right path with the least dangerous sections. Rockie is slowly coming along behind me, rescuing people who are stranded on the rocks or in danger of drowning. I think the Spooks are trying to tell me to slow down in my search for truth and take time to rescue those in need.

Believe me, if I were stranded on a rock, I would much prefer to see Rockie appear on his raft. Rockie wouldn't even try to interpret this dream for me. I knew what the message was. Since then I've tried to take time to smell the flowers and make room for others on my raft. My Aries self apparently still hasn't dropped the "me first."

Another dream I love was when I awoke with a line from "Top of the World" running through my head. I was sitting on a mountaintop watching a road race in the valley below. There were five little blue sports cars, all running in different directions at different speeds. You could see they would all end up at about the same spot in time. The song running through my head was, "I'm on top of the world, looking down on creation." Pretty obvious that even though we take different paths and don't all speed through life, the end will be the same. We all win.

One of the healers I read for called for Rockie to interpret two dreams that had her puzzled. In the first dream, she saw her father, who had been dead for many years. He looked really good, and people were lining up to give him money. Rockie told her that her father was receiving tribute for what he had done in his life. On the other side he was receiving what he had earned during his life and it was very positive. She should be happy for him and consider this a positive, happy, message from him.

The other dream had her in a restaurant with Barbara Walters and a dark person. They were having dinner and were really enjoying themselves. She wanted to know if this meant she would be as famous as Barbara Walters, or what? Rockie told her she would not be as famous as Barbara Walters. The dark person represented the negative side of her soul that she needed to work on. The light person represented people in everyday walks of life. She was not here for fame or money, but to help humanity in general. That would really make her happy. The restaurant indicated feeding others, but at a cost to her. Helping them also helps her advance in this lifetime.

## *The Meaning of Disturbing Dreams*

One of my most frequent and recurring dreams involves cooking for and feeding large groups of people. I'm always afraid I will run out of food and not have enough prepared for everyone. Also, the number of people expected to attend the dinner or party always keeps increasing. I awake apprehensive and afraid there won't be enough to go around. (Perhaps this is why I always cook too much, and why no one ever goes hungry!) I know logically it is not physical food I am dreaming about, but that is what is presented in the dream. Rockie has explained this to me repeatedly, but I still have the dream.

Another client called and needed Rockie's help with her dream. She was driving down a bumpy, winding road, trying to hurry home. It was dark and the road was next to a river that sparkled in the moonlight. After a long, hard drive, she finally arrived to find that her house was crumbling and falling apart.

Rockie told her the house represented her body, and that she was putting too much importance on the "house" instead of the path her life was taking in this lifetime. What she was searching for was beside her all the time, the spiritual side of her soul, which was represented by the sparkling river. He told her, "Don't put so much emphasis on the physical and material side of life." He did not know she was a model and was totally involved in her looks and money. I don't know if she heard the message or not.

Another of my clients kept dreaming that she or others around her had been shot and were dying. Rockie told her this did not signify an actual murder. He felt she was in the process of changing her own life and would be leaving some of these bad influences behind. They would be dead to her, therefore, or no longer in her life.

She had worked as a bartender and waitress in a very bad part of town and was seriously looking for work in another field and in a different part of town. This was not a warning that she would be shot, only to encourage her to move on with her own life. She did.

When Rockie interprets a dream, he doesn't know any of the personal details surrounding the person he is helping at the time. For this reason, it is interesting to him how accurate the interpretation was, when I later tell him what happened or what the background was.

Another of my regular clients called with a particularly upsetting dream. She does not believe in hunting or killing any creature. In her dream some hunters had come up to her house with what appeared to be a monkey, sitting in a car seat, that they had shot in the head. They said it was not a monkey, but a baboon. It looked at her and said "home" just before it died. She said Rockie told her the baboon is a scavenger, a user, and a taker. He was going "home." This meant someone around her who was not very spiritual was about to leave this earth. The message: Recognize there was nothing she could do to stop it, but just let that person go back to the other side and pray they will have learned something valuable from this lifetime.

She called a few days later and told me one of her acquaintances had gone "home." The description in the interpretation fit the person.

## Dream Symbols Are Unique

My dreams always have my body, the vehicle for the soul, represented by a car, bus, truck, or other vehicle. It's funny, but the vehicle depends on where I am at that time. Rockie says this is very typical; a vehicle usually means the soul, and a house means the body.

Each person has to help to determine what their own symbols are in the dream state. They can be very different for each of us. When Rockie talks to one of my clients to help determine the meaning of their dreams, he needs to ask a few questions to find out where they are and the direction their dreams might go, or what a particular item means to them in their waking life.

Symbols are what we usually refer to as the things we remember in dreams. They are representative of and stand for something important or significant to us. As mentioned, they vary for each individual, depending on their own experiences. Below is Rockie's list of dream symbols to help you understand your dreams. If you want additional information on various symbols, there are dream "dictionaries" on the market that include thousands of symbols and the interpretation by their authors. Keep in mind, however, another person's positive symbol might be a negative one for you. Rockie thinks a dog is a friend, but if you were attacked by a dog in a dream, your opinion might be different. Your own Spooks can help; listen to them.

| Symbol | Meaning |
|---|---|
| Accident | Usually a warning of some kind |
| Alarm | Alarm clock or phone ringing, siren; warning to wake up |
| Anger | Temper, frustration; learn to control yourself |
| Animals | Depends on your personal feeling about the dream animal |
| Back | Bearing burdens, physical strength |
| Bells | Reminder of something, listen |
| Babies | Birth of new ideas; new beginnings |
| Blood | Life, energy |
| Cancer | Something eating at you |
| Car | The vehicle used by your soul in this life; meaning determined by action of the car in the dream; out of gas, lack of energy (if it appears to be your own car, check it out mechanically—it may not by symbolic, but a warning about your car) |

| | |
|---|---|
| Cat | Independence, aloofness |
| Child | New ideas, psychic side of nature and abilities |
| Climbing | Moving toward a goal that is above you |
| Clothes | Level of consciousness; naked means exposed |
| Colors | See chapter on healings |
| Costume | Past life recall; actors on a stage in this life |
| Crying | Tears help to heal; crying out loud; let go |
| Curve | Rounding the bend; a change of life |
| Dancing | Spontaneous expression of inner self; in or out of step |
| Day | New day, facing toward the light |
| Death | May be actual contact with deceased person; end of something; dying out and leaving, not actual death |
| Disaster | Can be precognitive, but first see if this pertains to part of your current life situation |
| Dog | Friend, loyalty, obedient |
| Dreaming | To dream that you are dreaming can be associated with astral projection, especially if flying is involved |
| Ear | Related to hearing; listen, pay attention |
| Earthquake | Shake-up coming in your life, or it can be precognition |
| Escape | Wanting a way out of a situation |
| Eyes | Seeing, being aware, perception of something |
| Face | Face a situation, saving face; what you show the world |
| Falling | Typical feeling when pulled back into your body suddenly, just as you start to fall asleep; soul leaving the body at night |
| Feeding | Dispense truth, teach, as related to spiritual food |
| Feet | Understanding, balance |
| Female | Left side: Emotional, intuitive, receptive, gentle, artistic side of yourself; nurturing |
| Flag | Patriotism, standard |
| Flee, Run | Avoiding problems |

| | |
|---|---|
| Flowers | Note type of flower and color |
| Flying | Astral projection; rising above something, escape |
| Food | Spiritual or physical nourishment |
| Forehead | Clairvoyance and vision; the third eye location |
| Garden | Growth, nurturing, peaceful, Eden, security |
| Gift | Recognition, a talent, a present |
| Grass | Natural, peaceful, serene |
| Hair | Thoughts, attitudes you are carrying; messy is confused |
| Halo | Aura or spirituality |
| Hands | Right is giving or male, left is receiving or female |
| Head | Center of intellect, thoughts; head first; headstrong |
| Heart | Love and intuition; life force |
| Home | Security; place of origin, return to astral plane |
| Horse | Hard working, energetic, prophet or oracle |
| Illness | Dis-ease; emotional or physical problem |
| Injury | Hurt feelings, guilt or self-punishment; look for area of injury |
| Island | Isolation, loneliness |
| Killing | Killing part of self or behavior; letting go and changing |
| Knees | Weakness |
| Laughter | More carefree, happier, bright side of things |
| Legs | Direction or foundation of situation |
| Lion | Courage, the king of the beasts |
| Lips | Kiss, speaking, lips are sealed |
| Male | Masculine side, logical, active, intellectual, forceful; the right side of the body |
| Mirrors | Reflection of self; face your situation |
| Moon | Celestial body; spiritual ideas, reaching for |
| Mud | Neglect and confused situation; messy, dirty |
| Music | In harmony, divine forces, peacefulness |
| Night | Darkness, ignorance, unenlightened |

| | |
|---|---|
| Nose | Nosy, something smells, nose for news |
| Oasis | Refuge, safety |
| Ocean | Subconscious area, spiritual depth, deep |
| Pain | Physical or mental trouble or distress |
| Paralysis | Unable to move, frozen, immobile; no progress |
| Path | Path of life; look at surrounding symbols |
| Pool | Spiritual, look at condition of water; dark, clear, etc. |
| Pyramid | Antiquity and mystery; secrets |
| Raft | Unstable water, vehicle moving over depths, no controls |
| Rain | Cleansing process for the earth; spiritual nourishment |
| Rainbow | Promise, full spectrum of healing colors; hope |
| Restaurant | Place of nourishment for the soul, but at a price |
| Ring | Circle represents eternity; unity; completion |
| River | Spirituality of the highest; course of life; crossing over |
| Road | An individual's way or destiny; journey of the soul |
| Rocks | Obstacles in life, sturdy, and stable forces |
| Rope | Tied up; lack of freedom; roped in |
| Running | Getting out of a situation; run to or from something, hurry |
| Salt | Cleans, purifies; adds zest to life; wisdom |
| Sand | Shifting foundation, abrasive. Time symbol |
| Shampoo | Clean up, or clear one's thinking |
| Shield | Protection, defense |
| Skin | Individual's façade, exterior only |
| Smile | Approval; happiness |
| Smoke | Impending disaster, confusion |
| Snake | Enemy, deception, evil |
| Snow | Cold nature; spiritual growth needed; can show purity |
| Stab | Hostile acts or remarks, harm to self and others |
| Star | Achievement; high spiritual ideals; your light |
| Storm | Difficulty or trouble ahead; find safe harbor |
| Sun | Source of all energy; god or religious source |

| | |
|---|---|
| Swim | Spiritual activity; progress on top of water |
| Twins | Duplicity, two sides of something, two viewpoints |
| Thunder | Warning of impending storm |
| Underclothes | Hidden ideas, habits or attitudes; basis or under all |
| Vacation | Rest and relaxation; take a break |
| Walking | Moving ahead under your own power and direction |
| Water | Spiritual side of life; deep clear water is truth, murky or muddy water is no clear message, things confused and stirred up |
| Wind | Refreshing new ideas, feelings, and attitudes |
| Woods | Unknown area; subconscious, confusion |
| Yard | Front is what you present to the world, back is the hidden side or privacy area; the safe place for your house |

This is just a brief sample of various symbols and the meanings involved. If you really want to interpret your dreams, get additional information from someone who specializes in just dreams.

Keep in mind that symbols are unique as they apply to your situation. About twenty-five years ago, a good friend of mine had been having an unusual, recurring dream in which she was trying to catch a bus. She always arrived just as the bus left the curb and couldn't get the driver to stop. We puzzled over this weird dream and tried to see what she was missing or forgetting, but it made no sense until she was diagnosed with cancer. When the doctors performed surgery, they found she had two types of cancer invading her body at the same time. One type was in the female organs, which forced the doctors to do a complete hysterectomy. The other was in her lower intestines. They gave her just a 20 percent chance of living.

During her convalescence, she had the "bus dream" again. This time, when the bus pulled away from the curb, as it had in all of the other dreams, she thought, "Well, this is silly. I'll just hurry down the street and catch it on the return trip around the block." In her dream, she caught the bus on the return trip and got on. This was after dreaming of missing that bus for nearly a year.

Obviously, the bus was her symbol for the vehicle of her soul and what she kept missing was the cancer in her body. I don't know why her Spooks came up with a bus for her vehicle rather than just a little car, but it may be because she had always been overweight and felt big and awkward. She wasn't, but she thought so. It was also a learning experience for the soul. She chose not to accept either chemotherapy or radiation and treated herself with mega doses of vitamins. It worked for her. Last I heard, she was still alive and well, with no return of the cancer after over twenty-five years.

As you can see, repetitive dreams have an important message. If you can't understand them, find someone who can help you. The message may be intended to save your life. It can be your higher self, or soul, trying to get a message to your physical body. Ask for a repeat of a dream with variations until you figure it out. Your Spooks can give you the details in various forms until the message is clear.

---

### PSYCHIC TIP: HOW TO REMEMBER DREAMS

It is possible to start remembering your dreams, and many people recommend just writing down the first thought or recollection that is left in your mind as soon as you wake up. Even if it is in the middle of the night, keep a pencil and paper beside the bed and make a note. It will help you remember in the morning. There are many times I wish I had done this, especially when I know my Spooks just gave me a very important piece of information and it is totally gone in the morning.

If you make a point of telling yourself that you will remember your dreams and you will write them down, you will gradually start remembering them more clearly. Even the meanings will become pretty obvious. There are a multitude of books out on the subject of dream interpretations. Rockie has never read or used any of them. He just goes by what his guides are giving him in each individual situation.

That's good advice for you, too—trust your Spooks. Even if they are not as clear in your life as they are in mine, they communicate with you constantly about the things that are important in your life. You can hear them perhaps most clearly in your gut reactions to your experiences. Remember everything you love, hate, fear, or desire—these are the things that cause your gut reaction and may be involved in your dreams.

Try to interpret the meaning in your dreams using the symbols given in this chapter and the colors in a previous chapter. You may be surprised at how accurate the message is. It's like working out a puzzle, your own personal puzzle.

# CHAPTER TWELVE

# 9/11, Earthquakes, and Tsunamis

Many people have called me in the past few years, upset and concerned about the 9/11 disaster, earthquakes, tsunamis, and other natural and man-made disasters we have undergone during the past few years.

On the morning of the 9/11 attacks, I was awakened by a call from one of my clients who had been in the Marines and was listening to the TV. The phrase that ran through my head, over and over, apparently from the Spooks, was "Islamic Jihad." I don't consciously remember having ever heard that phrase before, and I tried to replace it with the name of Osama Bin Laden that had been in the news, but the Spooks wouldn't let me. I suppose they were insisting that I view this as the work of many, and not just one individual.

There is no doubt that the 9/11 attacks were as big or bigger than the attack on Pearl Harbor in 1941. It stunned America because we had gotten so used to the idea that we as a nation could not be hurt. We did not really understand the fear and response that other nations experienced regarding terrorists, and we learned how it feels when it hits home.

## *The Real Tragedy of 9/11*

The karma that had been set in motion by the action of the terrorists is the real tragedy. Each will have to pay for their part personally, and the souls who were injured have been pushed into the karmic wheel also. All souls involved in causing this event will have to answer for themselves, and there is no room for excuses on the soul plane. Reasons like, "They made me do it," "I had no choice, they would have killed my family," etc., just don't wash. All souls are accountable for their deeds and have to pay their debts.

If you consider some of the unbelievable atrocities individuals have caused on this earth you would find the whole idea of keeping track absolutely mind-boggling. Some souls have been responsible for many deaths, like the hijackers or Hitler, and God only knows how many others throughout history. It would be impossible for one individual soul to come back and lose their life enough times to repay each individual debt. That is what the "Akashic Records" are for. Every item is recorded to every last detail.

The karmic score, however, is not a soul for a soul, or a death for a death. Debts must be repaid only until the soul learns the karmic lesson needed to prevent repetition. After you think you have really learned and won't ever do "that again," the Spooks or your higher self give you one last test to see if you have really learned or are just assuming you are free of the problem by judging without the emotion. They throw in the emotion to see if you have really succeeded.

You know the old "Yes, but," story. It's the age-old excuse for ourselves and our poor choices. It doesn't work on the other side. You go back to step one again, and start over until you really learn. You can't con your higher self into believing you have learned; it just doesn't work.

The problem with those involved in perpetrating the Twin Towers disaster is that they thought they were doing what their religion and God wanted them to do, thanks to the teaching of their elders. They were just as hoodwinked by those in power as the Germans had been by Hitler. Eventually, they will see the effect the brainwashing had on their lives and not be as gullible in a future lifetime. They will still have to pay for their personal involvement, but they will be much less likely to be conned or sidetracked by others in future lives, and may in fact be very opposed to mind control. Incidentally, some people are deathly afraid of hypnosis because of the part they played in controlling the minds of others in this or an earlier lifetime.

The good part for those of us left grieving after 9/11 is the knowledge of the bravery, help, and thoughtfulness of so many who worked in the disaster, or who died as a result of it.

But understand: Each soul comes alone, and each soul leaves alone. The length of your life and the circumstances surrounding your death is predetermined before you are born. This is not arranged for us; we make the choices ourselves, and we agree with other souls to accomplish certain tasks and learn specific things. The moment you die is an agreement made with your guides and deeper soul and has a special meaning in the soul world for you alone.

No one died during the 9/11 attacks who hadn't already agreed to leave, therefore, in that manner on that day. It was a group learning experience and many who were affected and involved learned important lessons on that day. They still are learning. Some of the bravery displayed by those involved, especially those in the airplane over Pennsylvania and the firemen climbing the stairs in the Twin Towers—those who knew they would probably die—will never be forgotten. These are the legends our nation is famous for. These are the things we are so proud of.

The response from our country and our people after 9/11 was so overwhelming it will never be forgotten. Long after the pain of the disaster has been erased, the love, help, and caring that followed will be remembered. The Spooks say it will be similar to "Remember the Alamo" or "Remember Pearl Harbor" in scope and use.

## *There Is No Pain at Death*

At the time the 9/11 planes crashed into the Twin Towers, there was a drawing on the Internet that caught my attention and remains foremost in my mind to help explain the situation. In the drawing, an image of Jesus is shown over the towers with the smoke billowing out between his outstretched hands. Walking around on the clouds created by the smoke were all the souls who were dying in the disaster below. They were between his outstretched arms. They were happy, smiling, and knew where they were going. They had left immediately and were on their way home, many before the towers even collapsed. They were able to see the balance of the disaster from the other side without feeling the fear and pain we felt watching it happen.

This is not typical, but it can happen in disasters or events that would be too painful for the soul to need or want to endure. Your soul is able to leave the body every night when you go to sleep, so why not be able to leave when staying just a few more minutes would serve no purpose, except to teach "how to die"? We all already know how to do that. We have had to die and let go of the physical body many times during our incarnations. It is not new to our soul. The Spooks say the trauma of being born is actually much more painful and frightening. We just haven't been indoctrinated to fear birth, only death. That helps to keep us here, trying and learning!

## *Speak to the Departed*

The Spooks tell me that there is no pain at the moment of death. Just the peace and freedom that people who have out-of-body experiences tell us about. They don't feel the pain until they try to return to the body. There is no pain or fear on the other side. The only emotion we take with us is positive: happiness and love. Any soul who dies has only left their dirty old set of clothes behind, but now those souls continue to live on the other side. You will see them again. You can ask them any question you have, and yes they still love you and will help you in any way possible. You are part of their soul group, and your evolvement and continued progress is important to them.

You don't have to pray to them, because they are still with you. Say hi every day and listen or watch for their response. The response could be in a favorite book falling off a shelf, some question answered in an unexpected way, or in a dream. Sometimes it is just a greeting from behind your right shoulder that seems so real you want to spin around to see who is there. Remember the soul never dies, just the body.

Sometimes the memory will be brought back with full force due to a specific song being played, a particular aroma, or participating in something you shared with them in the past. This isn't an accident. It is their way of reminding you they are still with you, and love you.

## The Nature of Natural Disasters

Equally as serious and troublesome is the earthquake and tsunami disaster in the Indian ocean in December 2004. The final count of dead individuals will be over 250,000, which is a huge number to leave at any one time. The guides and helpers on the other side were really busy with the reception committees for so many, but each soul was greeted as though it was the only one that had arrived that day. Many who died during the disaster were very pleased to discover they had others in their immediate family taking the trip with them.

It is our inclination to blame God, nature, science, or a multitude of others for any natural disaster when it happens. This type of occurrence has been happening on this earth since the beginning of time, is not uncommon, and is necessary to the evolution of the planet. Our planet is an evolving organism, changing and reshaping itself all of the time.

When the tsunami had passed from the Indonesian area, a portion just under the sea was washed clean. It showed temples from a prior civilization that had been covered by silt on the ocean floor. Archeologists said it was the temple of the five pagodas, lost for a long time, but predicted to be found.

Humanity likes to live in the beautiful areas created by the "ring of fire," the outside edge or rim of the Pacific Ocean. It is an arc stretching from New Zealand, along the eastern edge of Asia and Japan, north and east across the Aleutian Islands of Alaska, and south along the coasts of North and South America.

Over 75 percent of the world's active and currently dormant volcanoes are located here, an area where earthquakes and volcanic eruptions are so prevalent. The recent earthquakes and tsunamis in Indo-China occurred within this area. Historically, the volcanic island of Krakatoa was once part of the island chain recently hit by the earthquake and tsunami. Krakatoa was totally destroyed in 1883 and the resulting tidal wave was over one hundred feet high. The tsunami is not a completely unheard of possibility for this area—just forgotten by current generations.

Similarly, the islands of Hawaii have been built by volcanoes. That's one way geography changes. Right now, something is forming just off the coast of Northern California and Oregon. There is daily earthquake activity in this area. The mound that is forming is now just 4,000 feet under the surface of the ocean and rising daily from the ocean floor, which is at a depth of 7,000 feet in that area. A new island?

The area known as the "ring of fire" has some of the most beautiful and picturesque areas on our planet, but it presents a danger for those who choose to live there. Many I have talked to would rather continue to live in the areas of greatest danger than move inland to an area less picturesque and maybe safer. This is the choice of each soul, and some think it is worth the trade off. It is again a choice. Would you live in the middle of a desert by choice if you could live on a tropical island? Most people pick the tropical island.

Some have no choice. One woman I read for was deathly afraid of earthquakes, but circumstances made it necessary for her to move to the Bay Area. She was very fearful of the move, but made it anyway. It helped her when the Spooks told her that if an earthquake hit, she wouldn't even be home. She would be out of state, visiting relatives. When the earthquake hit the Bay Area in 1989, the one that collapsed the freeway and did so much damage, she called me. She was in Wyoming visiting relatives and didn't intend to return to San Francisco. She felt she had survived this one and didn't want to tempt fate again. The Spooks didn't try to console her or talk her into moving back, so I said nothing.

## Sensing Danger

One of the women I read for always senses an earthquake before it happens. She can't really predict the area, just that it will happen in the next few days and how bad it will be. She is very accurate; the Spooks say she is very in tune with the physical earth. She actual feels the vibrations before it happens. One of our grandsons did the same thing when he was a small baby. He would scramble up to an adult and want to be picked up just before the tremor would hit—and he was only five months old.

Others have mentioned the eerie silence just prior to an earthquake. My mother used to sniff the air and say, "This is earthquake weather," just before a quake. I'm sure there is nothing in science to indicate certain weather precipitating an earthquake, but this was my mother's way of predicting it and letting us kids know. It really got our attention!

In the same way, animals and birds sense when an earthquake or disaster will strike. Dogs, for example, will be extremely nervous, barking or running around, then they will try to find a place to hide. This is similar to reports of elephants heading for high ground before the tsunami struck. Birds have also been known to disappear before a disaster or storm strikes. Somehow, they know. The lesson: watch animals and wildlife for clues that could save your life.

## *Disasters Pull Us Together*

The most outstanding thing about the whole Indonesian disaster is the manner in which the rest of the world joined together to help the victims. This was the largest combined effort for the good of mankind that had been undertaken up until this point. All the countries who sent money, medical teams, military help, and relief proved how great the power for good can be in this world.

Normally, of course, the only time we join together cooperatively is to wage war or behave destructively in some manner. We also have 20/20 hindsight and are quick to say "We should have" instead of "Why don't we . . .?" So many times in the past few years we could have stopped starvation, illness, or death and instead we chose to talk about it. The old axiom, actions speak louder than words, is so true.

The next time you are given the opportunity to help, actually get in and do something. It helps the world and helps your soul reach your ultimate goal.

## *The World: Mess or Status Quo?*

People always want to know what they can do personally to improve the state of the world, but at the same time they are willing to blame politics, religions, other countries, or the guy down the street. There is always plenty of blame to go around and we all want to spread it, but not share it.

Some people have asked if there is such a thing as a nation having a karmic debt. The Spooks say the country as a whole does not carry a debt, just the individuals involved in the crisis at the time. One reason is that the souls inhabiting all of the bodies in a country change completely every eighty years or so. And the national situation changes along with the change in people.

You might choose to return now to the country where you helped to cause the problem they are suffering from, to help change the understanding or direction of the entire nation. It would still be your personal choice, not a national one. Not all of the German people were involved in the holocaust and not all of the Japanese people flew planes over Hawaii.

If you review world history, you find that almost every country has been involved in some horrendous deed against another country in the past. You will also be reminded of our treatment of the Native Americans in our own country and hope we still don't owe on that one!

Some are seeking reparations for ancestors held in slavery. Consider the fact that one of the injustices the founding fathers of the United States were opposed to was the practice of indentured servitude existing at that time. They fought for their religious freedom and freedom from being indentured slaves in order to come here to create a free society and government, then some immediately forgot and brought black slaves here from Africa for their own financial gain, ignoring the sin of owning a slave. They apparently didn't learn enough to stop the behavior. If you take this one step further you find that the countries in Africa had for centuries been enslaving the defeated villages in many of their tribal wars. What goes around, comes around, but not for the entire nation. Just those involved in the debt.

Throughout recorded history, souls have seldom joined together with one common cause more important than their own personal soul improvement. One exception, according to the Spooks, is that the group of souls who were part of the Hundred Years' War reincarnated together and refused to fight in Vietnam, regardless of the consequences. The majority is still very judgmental of them; God help the politician who wants to run for office when his evasion of the draft comes out.

As a nation or group we are seldom brave enough to stand up for each other and band together on any issue. If you consider the multitude of issues currently tearing the United States apart such as the current war, stem cell research, abortion, fundamentalism, the clash of religion and politics, and our inability to solve even our own problems, how can we expect the United Nations or any group currently on earth to do any better? The Spooks say people in glass houses shouldn't throw stones, and we certainly live in large, very fragile, glass houses.

## The Coming Cleansing

Many feel the earth is heading into a serious period of change and feel the physical changes are already starting to occur. The Spooks say that this is a normal process and the earth periodically repairs and cleanses itself. We have read and studied about the ice ages, the threat of a change of the poles, and seen some very graphic movies with trick photography that make this seem quite possible. The big question is, will the earth completely cleanse itself next time, to the point that the human race goes the way of the dinosaurs?

Our lack of concern for the ecology of this planet and our interest in money and power make this seem possible.

## Y2K: Mass Fear

Prior to New Year's Day in 2000, I had many calls from people wanting to know if they should stockpile food, water, and other supplies needed for survival, in response to the Y2K scare. Many were going out and buying anything being recommended on the Internet.

One night in September 1999, my Spooks awakened me at about 2:00 AM. I went into the living room and raised my hands, palms up toward the heavens and asked for guidance on the Y2K question. I was told very clearly, "Y2K already came and went and nobody noticed. You are on the wrong calendar and the concern is false." This was a big relief to me, since I had been telling all of my clients to ignore the warning and the many attempts to frighten them. It was all just hype. I needed some verification from my Spooks and they gave it that night. I had become concerned that I was not giving people the right information and could cause them harm if I was wrong.

As we all now know, Y2K really did pass without incident, but for a short time before the date I questioned my Spooks too. When everyone around you is fearful, you begin to doubt yourself.

The mass fear and hysteria averted may help people to be a little less willing to jump on the mass media hype like a herd of thoughtless animals. A benefit would be that the entire hype proved to be false, and just an advertising gimmick to sell anything to anyone. An additional benefit was that people actually started to be concerned for each other instead of wondering how much ammunition they needed to stockpile to prevent their neighbors from taking their food! It is reminiscent of the bomb shelters that mushroomed in back yards during the start of the cold war. We were young married people and everyone was talking about building or having a bomb shelter. If you weren't planning for that horrible end, others thought you just didn't love your family. It also reminds me of the atomic bomb drills in elementary school. We were taught to hide under our desks and cover our faces! How useless that would have been in a real disaster. Makes you wonder how much we've really learned, or forgotten.

## *To Improve the World: Identify Your Purpose*

Your life purpose goes back to the age-old question: "Why am I here?" The next question will be "How am I supposed to do that?" Then, "Why?" If I could answer those questions for you, I wouldn't be here either. I would have progressed beyond this plane! We all have planned our specific goals and lessons to learn in each lifetime. Some are very profound, some very mundane, but it depends on who you are talking to today. What you think is a simple, foolish goal might be an overwhelming accomplishment for another soul. Don't judge since you don't know the background and you have not "walked in those moccasins."

You can help yourself discover your most important goals by identifying the things that are karmic to you personally: anything you love, hate, fear, or desire. Love is fine if it is not a selfish thing that only involves your own needs and gratification.

"You are to love others as you love yourself, and do unto others as you would have them do unto you." This is known as the Golden Rule, or the greatest commandment. It is also common sense. Too many of us are only looking out for ourselves. Our ultimate goal is and should be higher than that.

## Love

One woman I read for was pregnant with her fifth child when I first talked to her. The older four children were from two previous marriages and one short-term relationship—five children with four different fathers. She had been making some very poor choices and was now responsible for the futures of five children. In various readings she came to realize she had been trying to force permanent relationships by having children to try to maintain the hold on the various companions. It obviously was not working. She loved her children and didn't want to release custody of any of them. Through readings and serious introspection, she completely changed her life. She went back to school with federal and state aid and became a registered nurse. She is now doing very well financially, the five children are in their early teens, and she is still single.

Do you know what the current question is? You guessed it, "Will I ever find a love of my own?" She will, but not until the youngest child is eighteen. She still just doesn't trust men or her ability to recognize love. She was confusing love with desire, sex, and control, and doesn't want to get back on that roller coaster. Her self-image has improved to the point that she believes she is someone worth loving, so she will find someone worth loving.

## Hate

Hate is something you need to work on. Try to understand exactly what evokes the feelings of hatred. Is this against an individual or a particular situation? See what you can do to change the situation that causes this feeling. Can you learn more to understand the background or basis of this situation? Sometimes, if you really hate something, you will be required to wear it or have one of your loved ones become involved in that situation.

This reminds me of the man I read for who hated gays and everything about them until his son admitted he was gay. He didn't change his attitude overnight. First he needed to accept the possibility and the fact. He had to learn more about gays and then be willing to accept this for his son. The other alternative was to cut off all contact with his only son and lose him in this lifetime. He didn't want to lose the son, and he gradually learned to accept his choice.

The main lesson was to learn tolerance. If he didn't do it in this lifetime, then he would be faced with the same or similar problems in another. He didn't have to live that life now, but he had agreed to start to understand it. He really did learn it was okay to love a gay son and not be ashamed of him.

## Fear

Our fears are karmic and can be pretty silly or very crippling, depending on how intense or serious they are. My frogs are pretty much silly and not very important. Others have fears that really restrict their life. My mother was deathly afraid of flying her entire life and missed many opportunities because of her refusal to even discuss the problem. When she flew to Hawaii with us when she was 71, she discovered she loved it. In her words, "Flying above the clouds was like the view from heaven. It was beautiful and we were as free as the birds." I'm sure she only agreed to go because she thought her life was over and she didn't care if she got killed. Several cocktails later, she loved it. Face your fears.

Then be willing to try something to confront them. You may end up surprised, like Mom.

## Desire

Desires are our needs and wants exaggerated way beyond necessity. Most of our needs are provided, some of our wants, and a few of our desires. The problem with letting our personal desires get out of hand is it leads to greed, and a need for power and control. Living by the Golden Rule keeps greed and power-hungriness under control. When you realize that, through the Law of Return and karma, everything you put out comes back to you, it will make you think twice, because this includes not only the good things, but also all of the selfish, bad things we do. Think about it!

Note that this is not preaching, just good sense. It is so neat when you change your behavior and start seeing the changes around you. For instance, when I bought a Lotto ticket the other night, the clerk didn't charge me enough. I pointed that out to him, gave him the other dollar and was really surprised when he said, "That's right—if you try to cheat me out of the money, karma won't let you win the Lotto." Judging by his position, clothing, and attitude, this was totally unexpected! I was pleasantly surprised and agreed 100 percent. (I still didn't win. Oh, well!)

How can you make even one person give up their search for wealth and power? It seems almost impossible when you multiply those negative desires by the millions of individuals who still have these goals and seem to have lost sight of their original intention. Our souls are advancing in some ways, but we may be missing the big picture. Souls don't come seeking wealth and power on earth, but our good intentions and plans can be closed off or detoured by the choices we make or sometimes by the choices of others near us. Remember that free will and choice are always active. We are not forced to do anything, and so sometimes our good intentions are channeled away from the original goal.

Back to our purpose on earth: I'm too old to be personally involved in the war in Iraq, but I have grandsons who are in the U.S. Army and Air Force there. I also have a granddaughter who has a doctorate in chemistry currently working in stem cell research. Another grandson has his doctorate in planetary geology; maybe he will be the one to learn the correct procedures to predict earthquakes. Another wants to be a senator and will probably make it in twenty years with that serious goal at so young an age. Another is working on his master's degree in psychology to try to help souls understand and live with the decisions they make.

Each is concerned for the good of mankind, but each is also involved in their own personal goals or the tests they have set up to learn from. I don't have the wisdom to suggest that any soul change the path they are taking in this life. I have enough trouble with my own path. We have to remember not to judge until we walk a mile in another soul's moccasins. I do counsel my callers to accept and understand the choices they have made.

We have to remember that this earth is a learning center and, as I've stated before, some consider it the "Insane Asylum of the Universe," because the souls who have most to learn choose or are strongly encouraged to return to this plane, over and over, until they get it right. Many I've talked to just hope this is their last incarnation on this planet and never want to return. This has also become part of my own personal goal, but the marking in my palm says I'll be back. Maybe through necessity, maybe through choice or to help some other souls, but as McArthur said, "I shall return."

Damn! Oh, well.

---

### PSYCHIC TIP: IDENTIFY YOUR PURPOSE
### IN THIS GO-ROUND

Remember, the things you need to work on the most are your own karmic problems. These include anything you love (to the point of ignoring all else), hate, fear, or desire. These are things that involve your purpose in this life.

For example: If you feel very strongly about child abuse, would never do it, feel nauseated when you hear or read about it, etc., you can get involved in some area to help stop, counsel, teach, or prevent it. Choose to volunteer or be on a board of directors for a group that works with this problem. Don't just talk about it. Contribute your time and money to help. Actions speak louder than words.

Alternatively, if you understand and are concerned about global warming and disasters, do all you can personally do to reduce gas emissions, recycle as much as possible, and encourage others to do the same. Buy and try one of the new hybrid or electric vehicles.

Think about what you love, hate, fear, and desire. Then act based on your observations, and you'll be fulfilling your purpose.

---

**PSYCHIC TIP: LOVE THE EARTH**

Appreciate the beauty and special features our earth has. Say so and think peace, love, and help to the earth every day. Some say it is too late, but I don't think so. Remember: Our faith can move mountains, even a mountain of trash.

Let's prove the harmonic convergence can happen every day from every one of us. If we save our beautiful earth, we save a place for our grandchildren to go to school and learn their lessons in the future. We owe that to them and to ourselves. Wouldn't you like to be part of the amazing civilization that stopped the problems and turned it all around? We can as a group!

The key word is "Choice." That doesn't mean we condone it or ignore the hard lessons. Just learn from them and improve our own personal attitude and future choices for ourselves and the earth. It is our earth and our future.

Remember the "I am" therapy and continue to use it! "I am healthy, I am happy, I am full of energy." Doing so will, quite naturally, improve the condition of the earth as well.

## To Write to the Author

If you wish to contact the author or would like more information about this book, please write to the author in care of Llewellyn Worldwide and we will forward your request. Both the author and publisher appreciate hearing from you and learning of your enjoyment of this book and how it has helped you. Llewellyn Worldwide cannot guarantee that every letter written to the author can be answered, but all will be forwarded. Please write to:

Alice Rose Morgan
℅ Llewellyn Worldwide
2143 Wooddale Drive, Dept. 0-7387-0936-0
Woodbury, Minnesota 55125-2989, U.S.A.
Please enclose a self-addressed stamped envelope for reply, or $1.00 to cover costs. If outside U.S.A., enclose international postal reply coupon.

Many of Llewellyn's authors have websites
with additional information and resources.
For more information, please visit our website at
http://www.llewellyn.com

## LLEWELLYN ORDERING INFORMATION

### Order Online:
Visit our website at www.llewellyn.com, select your books, and order them on our secure server.

### Order by Phone:
- Call toll-free within the U.S. at 1-877-NEW-WRLD (1-877-639-9753). Call toll-free within Canada at 1-866-NEW-WRLD (1-866-639-9753)
- We accept VISA, MasterCard, and American Express

### Order by Mail:
Send the full price of your order (MN residents add 7% sales tax) in U.S. funds, plus postage & handling to:

**Llewellyn Worldwide**
**2143 Wooddale Drive, Dept. 0-7387-0936-0**
**Woodbury, Minnesota 55125-2989, U.S.A.**

### Postage & Handling:

**Standard** (U.S., Mexico, & Canada). If your order is:
$49.99 and under, add $3.00
$50.00 and over, FREE STANDARD SHIPPING

AK, HI, PR: $15.00 for one book plus $1.00 for each additional book.

**International Orders** (airmail only):
$16.00 for one book plus $3.00 for each additional book

*Orders are processed within 2 business days.*
*Please allow for normal shipping time. Postage and handling rates subject to change.*